Barge Country

Also by John Liley
Journeys of the *Swan*
France – the Quiet Way
Inland Cruising Companion

BARGE COUNTRY

An Exploration of the Inland Waters
and Great Rivers of the Netherlands

John Liley

STANFORD MARITIME   LONDON

Stanford Maritime Limited
Member Company of the George Philip Group
12–14 Long Acre   London WC2E 9LP
Editor Phoebe Mason

First published in Great Britain 1980
Copyright © John Liley 1980

Designed by Sue Cawson

Filmset in 10/12 Apollo
Printed in Great Britain by
BAS Printers Limited
Over Wallop, Hampshire

ISBN 0 540 07179 X

British Library Cataloguing in Publication Data
Liley, John
    Barge country.
    1. Netherlands – Description and travel
    2. Inland navigation – Netherlands
    I. Title
    914.92′04′7   DJ41
    ISBN 0-540-07179-X

Acknowledgements

Short sections of this book, on the purchase of *Secunda* and the route through Belgium, have previously appeared in *Motor Boat and Yachting*. I am indebted to the Editor, Dick Hewitt, for permission to reproduce them here. I also wish to thank Hugh Potter of *Waterways World*, and Alex McMullen, Eric Coltham, the Netherlands and Belgian National Tourist Offices, T. Thompson, Raab Karcher GmbH and Theo Kampa for additional photographs.

Contents

Arthur

There were nights on board *Arthur* when the stove burned so fiercely you could smell people's trousers charring. To sit before such a blaze was a boyhood dream of mine; to explore the European waterways another. In my previous book *France – the Quiet Way* I explained how the ambition can be realised, how a simple yet characterful vessel like *Arthur* may be purchased and taken into Continental waters.

Arthur was such a barge, and he came from the North, the cloth-capped tripe-eating part of England I was born in myself. The name gave him away, for Lancashire lads and Yorkshire boatmen christened their craft with abrupt, masculine titles. This matter-of-fact approach was demonstrated by several scars on *Arthur*'s bow, the result of shouldering into locks on the Leeds & Liverpool Canal and colliding with the stonework at the other end. It was the custom to do this, the steerer leaping off like some *kamikaze* pilot who has suddenly remembered his granny. This enabled him to close the gates and wind the sluices while working up the canal on his own.

Since those rumbustious days *Arthur* had been basically converted, with a capacious, cheery saloon over part of the hold and a low deck across the remainder. Crouching figures could be found under this, in search of, or upon, the lavatory, which was at the stern. The old boatman's cabin was under the bow, with the stove that first enticed me. Bench seats faced this stove, while behind them two bunks could be entered through a sort of picture frame arrangement in the panelling. I had special mattresses made,

regardless of expense, to fit the unique lozenge-shaped spaces these frames enclosed. A friend got an expert to make them, of extra-thick foam, and to lie upon one after a hard day's exertion at the tiller was like hurling oneself upon the concrete surface of a motorway. Thickness and price are plainly not the criteria of mattresses, and I recommend all purchasers to grill the manufacturers before ordering.

At the back of *Arthur* (to use English canal terminology) there also stood a BMC diesel, a replacement for the cast-iron museum piece that was once installed. Above this was the steering position, at an open tiller.

An important distinction must now be made. *Arthur* was not one of the long, brightly decorated craft that worked around the English Midlands for a century and a half. Those are *narrow boats*, seventy feet long and seven wide. *Arthur*, sixty feet by fourteen, was of a type known as a 'short boat' on the Leeds & Liverpool Canal. In waterway circles, any vessel of this nature, with a beam of fourteen feet or over, may be correctly termed a 'barge'.

It was because of this difference, and the narrowness of some locks in Northamptonshire, that *Arthur* came around the coast to London. That voyage, and the one following across the English Channel, are also described in *France – the Quiet Way*. We stayed in France for two long seasons, wandering to and fro across the country and joined by groups of friends who came and went by train. People who travel by car are a hopeless liability on a barge journey, since you spend half the time plotting the recovery of their

Lemmer: the town centre. (Theo Kampa)

A French lock, capable of receiving the standard 350 ton péniche *of the central canals. At 19 metres overall,* Arthur *is half the length and also some 70 centimetres less in beam than the* péniche's *full 5 metres.*

vehicles; but there can be crises whatever the transportation.

Our own occurred as I returned from a brief visit to England. We had planned to take *Arthur* back there at the end of summer and were vaguely headed in that direction, but in the meantime a canal had been closed for repair. Michael Streat, to whom I had recently sold a share in the boat, discovered the news too late to warn me. I tried to rejoin him in the heart of France, one moonless night, after taking a taxi, costing seven pounds, to a place where *Arthur* wasn't. I next walked nine miles of towpath, pausing to hold a glow-worm against the map in a forlorn attempt at reading it. By then it was one o'clock in the morning, and after knocking up a hostile lock-keeper, I lay beneath the hedge in my best suit, with a duty-free bottle of brandy as the only compensation for a raging thirst and the absence of lunch, tea or supper. A thunderstorm crackled around the horizon, a herd of cows tramped across the field to look at me, while various smaller animals snuffled and argued in the grass across the water.

In the morning I received a message left by Bob, one of the crew. He had come over to meet me by bicycle, and on the pannier had brought another bicycle, a folding one. Bikes were our normal transport for provisioning and rendezvous; we used to spend more time repairing them than looking after the boat. The folding one was a particular favourite, presented when I left the Editorship of *Motor Boat and Yachting*. When I failed to arrive at the expected time, Bob had allowed himself to be drawn into a drunken gathering. On pedalling away later he forgot about the second bicycle on the back, and passing too close to the only stationary car in the district had scratched it rather badly. He tried to explain to some local children, but his French was bad, his nerve broke and he fled, never able to return.

All this I gathered later. The message, left at another lock-keeper's (for I had knocked at the wrong house), merely told me where *Arthur* was, and that I might get there on a nonexistent bicycle. The boat was thirty kilometres away. I took a lift in an early milk lorry, calling at various small-holdings along the way. I remember the driver dropping his fag ash into a pile of clotted cream as he reached across to open the door. Finally a Clochemerle character in an ancient Bugatti took me to the boat. After all that, it seemed perfectly reasonable to change our minds and head for the Netherlands. And that is what we did.

Around the stove: a group of friends in Arthur's *bow cabin.*

The Moselle – Introduction

It is easy to spread out a map of Europe, wave a Napoleonic arm across it, and say you will be in Rotterdam for tea. From the city of Nancy, it was to take us four weeks. The big commercial barges go faster, but it would be a mighty financial lure that made me hasten down the valley of the Moselle.

This is one of ten routes across the northern French border. Most of them soberingly dull, though the Meuse has a moody magnificence and the Rhine from Strasbourg the feeling of being carried down an escalator on which the throttle spring has broken. But the Moselle is the one that generates the rhapsodies. Tamer than the Rhine, less inclined than the Meuse to rolling mist or flooding, this is one of the sparkling waterways of Europe.

The early reaches give only an inkling of the glories further north. As far as Thionville, the view is of gravel pits and heavy industry, with the odd snatch of scenery thrown in. Such curiosities as the stub end of a Roman aqueduct at Ars alternate with swathes of power lines. Pont-à-Mousson has a good wall and a view of its industry from a nearby hill, while it is well worth stopping at Metz, with its lofty cathedral scorched within by wine-red glass. Metz, an illustrious city, stands just off the main navigation and the best mooring is among a confusion of streams at its centre, reached by a short branch above the town lock. Failing this, the dreary commercial port will have to do, in the final stages of the lock cut.

From here to Thionville much of the route is along artificial canal, its banks gnawed and eroded by wash. This is an enlarged version of the CAMIFEMO, the Canal des Mines de Fer de la Moselle, and there is a background of furnaces and mechanical toil.

By *Arthurian* standards these are wide, deep waters, with locks far removed from the clog-worn affairs of the Leeds & Liverpool. Even the standard 350 ton barge of central France seems trivial by comparison. Each chamber can take many such vessels, the ubiquitous bluff-nosed *péniches*, and we would often float down with several of them, each hanging casually from a single rope as the water dropped. Occasionally we might move the noose to a further bollard, recessed in the wall, and sometimes, if there was another

Remains of the Roman aqueduct at Ars, where it once spanned the Moselle valley.

vessel ahead, we would also attach a bow line, lest her wash beset us. Since all these locks are electrically operated, there is little else to do except wave to the keeper on leaving.

Hagondange and Thionville are regions of glowing skies and mighty reverberations in the dusk. Algerian steelworkers with weary faces wait at the bus stops. The waters are soupy, while patches of scrubby grass mingle with the steel and reinforced concrete. It is said that when Germany annexed Lorraine in 1871 it was in order to obtain a strategic frontier, and that the iron ore deposits were secured unwittingly; but they sustained Germany throughout the Great War, before the Armistice afforded France the return of Lorraine. It may be symbolic of the antagonism that lingered that the CAMIFEMO, built later, could be entered only from the direction of Nancy. The stretch of river across the border stayed shallow and unnavigable.

These remaining sections of the Moselle are held to have been used in Roman times, conjuring up a vision of figures in togas bouncing down the rapids on rafts; but in 1964 the International Moselle Waterway was opened, navigable all

The Moselle and a section of the Rhine, south of the Ruhr. The River Saar is expected to become fully navigable by 1984, with eight new locks between Saarbrucken and the connection with the Moselle.

A mooring near the centre of Metz, reached by branching off from the main navigation.

the way to the Rhine. France, Germany and Luxembourg jointly subscribed 780 million Deutchmarks, in one of the first essays in cooperation within the European Community. Fourteen locks were built, great boxes of concrete each capable of passing a 3,320 ton load. The mother company, formed to supervise the operation, and theoretically to be disbanded at the end of it all, is still entangled today in the hassles over land rights and compensation. Since the waterway has already approached its maximum capacity, there will be more entanglements to come, as the locks are to be duplicated to allow for further growth. The traffic passes in barges that make *Arthur* seem like a dinghy, and much is in push-tows, with a tug lashed astern of a raft of lighters. The International Moselle is a classic case of traffic being

attracted because a highway is there, and although the main object was to connect the steelworks of Lorraine with the Rhine and Dutch ports, several further harbours have become established along its length.

It might be supposed that a fine valley has been wrecked by modern intrusions, but there are remarkably few signs. Indeed, as *Arthur* passed down the concrete canyon at Thionville and entered the International Section, the countryside was already perking up. The first terraced slopes appeared, and a crest of woodland. Following a large pusher tug, in which the helmsman sat in a glass eyrie, equipped with opera glasses so that he could see what the bow was doing, we left Königsmachern Lock and headed for Apach, the frontier with Luxembourg and Germany.

Industry at Pont-à-Mousson

Crossing the Border

Connoisseurs of the Customs official have the opportunity of meeting three widely differing types at Apach. The first, who is French, occupies a cabin set back from the lockside and it is tempting to slip by without calling on him. In our own case, tucked in behind a push-tow and descending into the abyss, this seemed quite possible had not the lock-keeper himself, somewhat beyond the line of duty I thought, indicated that we must take along the ship's papers.

Captains who suffer from vertigo are advised to carry a hardy crew member who can be sent, like some Victorian toddler up a chimney, on the awe-inspiring climb up a lockside. He needs either a big pocket or a firm set of teeth in which to clutch the *papiers*, particularly on reaching the tricky overhand where the ladder stops and the lock kerb begins. There is sometimes a horrid little handhold set into the lock at this point, a collecting point for rainwater and the keeper's tea leaves. There is also a tendency for the knees to strike the chin as the actual summit is negotiated. Those with foresight will have hopped off the boat before the water begins to drop, although *papier* requirement is not often signified at this stage. In either event, there will always be a long journey back.

In France travellers used to be, and in some cases still are, provided with a Green Card upon entry to the country. Onto this particulars of the vessel would be entered, either from the ship's registration papers, if she was indeed registered, or from a handy piece of cardboard obtainable from the Royal Yachting Association in Woking. As I write, the Green Card

has been discontinued, except in places, of which Calais is one, where the news has been slow to filter through. Either way, it is vital to obtain some evidence of the date a vessel enters France, or she may be deemed to have stayed over six

Pusher tug with two barges and a total capacity of over 3,000 tons, working upstream near Remich, Luxembourg.

One of the last steam locomotives, by the riverside near the frontier with France. Steam haulage survived in Germany until the mid-1970s.

months. At this the Authorities will impose a swingeing import duty.

All this passed through my mind as I approached the cabin. Through a bizarre series of blunders I had acquired a *tryptique*, a book of forms normally given to people who tow their boats behind cars. It had been foisted upon me in France by a firm of *transporteurs*, agents towards whom local Customs officials may waft you, to save themselves five minutes' work. The work involved is placing the vessel in bond for the winter. This allows another duty-free period

the following year; but the fees that a *transporteur* charges, compounded from formulae entirely of his own design, make one wonder if importation might not be cheaper after all. My purpose then was to get an out-of-date Green Card and the wrong document duly authorized. I need not have worried. It was a hot, sticky afternoon, the rubber stamp rose and fell in the hand of an automaton, and I merely slipped the papers beneath it to record our departure.

For those intending to call at a Luxembourg port, and all the ports on the next forty kilometres of river are on the Luxembourg side, there is a jetty below the lock. Here the Luxembourger Customs may be visited, two gentlemen in AA patrolmen's uniform perspiring in a caravan beside the main road. They told me to clear off, more or less.

This was a bad preparation for the German Customs, who have a black gunboat just downstream. They roar alongside just as you have decided to celebrate the crossing, focusing their binoculars at point-blank range. Ours were not impressed by the RYA paper, nor the *tryptique*, nor by the departure of the entire crew in search of its cameras, in order to record a steam locomotive that came rolling up beside the river bank. There are many regulations concerning pleasure boating in Germany, particularly if your vessel is over '15 tons', a vague but ominously low figure. Certificates of competence, of sea and weatherworthiness, of exemption or otherwise from pilotage, all hang heavily in the air. It is a good plan to carry lots of papers on board, certifying skills of almost any kind, and they should look as formal and complicated as possible. In the end our insurance document filled the bill, with its impressive array of gothic typefaces and dozens of clauses. Fortunately, as I now realize, none of the officers understood English or French, while the member of our crew who had some German managed completely to forget it. They left, as a parting gesture depositing another wad of forms, concerning the purchase of fuel. These seemed so terribly complex that, like others before me, I resolved to bunker in Luxembourg.

The Moselle from Apach to Koblenz

After a summer in France, Both Germany and Luxembourg provide a cultural shock. Not only is the name of the river spelled differently – it is the Mosel to Germans – but habits in eating and shopping are greatly at odds with the French. Shops in France often stay open on Sunday; those in Germany rarely do. Fresh bread can be acquired in France almost around the clock, perhaps because it lasts no time at all. German bread is not baked at weekends, but it has the consistency of cake, looks like congealed lava and lasts forever. Luxembourg bread, in my judgement, is feeble in every respect.

There are of course restaurants to visit, and if arriving at a weekend, like ourselves, foolishly unprovisioned, these may have to be patronized. A maddening characteristic of Remich, the first major town on the Luxembourg side, is the widespread insistence upon Luxembourg's own currency, which is understandable, or that of Belgium, which is miles away. The coins of Germany, from just across the river, are generally rejected.

Remich is otherwise jolly and neat, with restaurants and shops set back across a wide and very public quay. The moorings are for pleasure boats only, save for a stretch with 'No Parking' signs, reserved for river steamers. On Sunday afternoons half the population strolls along the quay to scrutinize its visitors, while the other half goes water-skiing. The river here can be bedlam, with ski-boats whirring like hornets, flailing in and around each other, and across the bows of the pusher tugs that cruise by imperiously.

My view of Germans, until then one of awe at their efficiency and sense of order, was modified here by the sight of a large but elderly motor barge of that nation staggering through the throng with a load of coke. After a little shuffling, she was tied to the very signs that prohibited it, and a figure sent ashore with a bicycle and shopping bag. As is always the way on such occasions, a white steamer immediately appeared, looking like a wedding cake on a saucer, to whistle and hoot for the berth. She was shortly joined by the friendly black Customs launch, which started to agitate through a loudhailer. After about ten minutes of this, an old lady appeared on the bridge of the barge, shook her fist at the tormentors and retired below again. This process was repeated a quarter hour later, by which time the cyclist, pedalling briskly, came weaving back through the merrymakers on the quay. As he jumped aboard the ropes were flicked away, and the lady switched from a defensive posture to a positive tirade as the barge gave a slow *ker-chonk* and moved off. She was still at it as they disappeared around the corner, and the patrol vessel shrank away.

The patron saint of barge people has long been Saint Nicholas, and on both Rhine and Moselle there are numerous statues and shrines. There is one such at Remich, set high up in an archway at the back of the quay, and this signifies not only that this section of the Moselle must have been navigable, after a fashion, long before the recent works, but that the river has been wider at this point, and probably washed quite closely to the gateway where Saint

THE MOSELLE FROM APACH TO
KOBLENZ

Vineyards at Trittenheim

Nicholas stands. In the days when the river was shallow and fast, and particularly where it rushed through rapids and tight bridges such as the one downstream at Trier, the protection of the saint was often invoked. There remains a strong religious element today, and at the start of a voyage German captains may still be seen almost formally putting on a peaked cap with the words *In Gottes Namen* – 'In God's Name'. Traditionally the start of a voyage is signified also by three strokes on the ship's bell, and this is still sometimes done.

Wine makes an entry at Remich, a sparkling type, St Martin; and there is more produced at Wormeldange and Grevenmacher, further downstream, before the big, daunting port of Mertert and the smaller, traditional one at Wasserbillig.

It is common to lie outside a group of *péniches* at Wasserbillig, since the inviting space at the quayside is again kept free for steamers. There are two hazards in the arrangement: slavering hounds, which chase the shoregoer across the intervening ships; and the fact that barge traffic can sometimes pass very close, especially late at night. A small riding light, mounted on the extreme outer corner of the accommodation, is an antidote for the one, but the dog problem can only be dealt with by pointed looks towards the owners, raised from their telly-watching slumber by the clatter of feet on their decks and the growls of a beast in hot pursuit.

Wasserbillig itself is a cheerful spot on the junction with a smaller river, the Saur. From this point onwards the left bank of the Moselle is German also. There is a Customs post on the Wasserbillig quay, a wooden shed which was locked when we called.

A further river enters the Moselle a little distance down, the inviting but unnegotiable River Saar. This is another that is navigable only in its higher reaches, those that lie south of the French border, although registration at Saarbrucken on the frontier itself has long been an advantage for barge captains, since it gives their craft a dual nationality. This allows them to accept loads in either country, free of hindrance. Elsewhere in Europe, even within the Common Market, a barge may only take a return load back towards her country of origin, and freewheeling or 'tramping' is not permitted.

The Saar is now receiving the same treatment as the Moselle. Eight locks are being built, at an even greater cost, and the river should be open all the way by 1985.

In both the Luxembourg and German parts of the Moselle, there is a charge at each lock, unless occupied by a steamer or a barge in which case the barge captain pays and any 'yacht' may pass through for nothing. At the time of our descent in *Arthur* the price at each lock was ten marks. This was not expensive to a German yachtsman (a rare species, since he has to comply with all manner of rules and hold a certificate that the foreign visitor escapes); but it seemed a high price to the British. The skids were under Sterling, the exchange rate already on its catastrophic descent from the recent memory of ten Deutschmarks for every pound. It was to fall to less than four. At that sort of price it is tempting to hang about for a barge, but there are often two of them, which neatly fill a lock, and the wait can be a long one. I had read that if a barge was expected in the opposite direction, we could be let down for nothing as the keeper prepared the lock, but our claims on the matter were not respected and we had to pay.

The German locks have that distinguishing note of efficiency and order. Traffic signals indicate readiness (and binoculars are a valuable means of reading them), while there are often instructions on loudspeakers. At *Arthur*'s first, just before Trier, the voice seemed to come from out of the chamber itself. 'Hammelfleischwurstundspiegeleimit grunersalat', it appeared to say; 'I demand to see the manager'. Glancing coyly towards the big control cabin, as if to say 'Very well, thank you', I hoped that the message was not for us. Alas, it was repeated, twice, so

Saint Nicholas' gateway at Remich, Luxembourg, with painting of the boatpeople's patron saint.

that in the end a volunteer was sent along the lockside to convey our unconditional surrender. Once again, while mentally still in France, it was a shock to find a race so near at hand doing things so very differently. Experiences like this sent me off to German classes at night school the following winter, the feeling of inadequacy being heightened when our envoy returned to say that the lock-keeper was merely asking if we wanted to use the water hose.

Mosel hoses are another adventure. Put a coin in a slot, and you receive a cubic metre of water, whether you want that amount or not. *Arthur*'s tank held a paltry twenty gallons, which we made last for several days by providing an almost unworkable tap. Twenty gallons is one-tenth of a cubic metre only, and we had the ludicrous experience of directing most of the supply back into the river.

Another odd feature of the Mosel locks is the manner in which they are negotiated by the push-tows. When descending the river they are prevented from striking the lower gates by a thick steel cable placed across the chamber; but once they have moored, a swinging arm is lowered across the lock to attach itself magnetically to the cable end and lift it clear. The tow then moves forward an extra metre or so, the helmsman watching the position and the work of

Bernkastel (below)
Cochem (facing page)

the deckhands through binoculars. Even the Mosel authorities have to learn by their mistakes: the locks in the German and Luxembourg sections are a fraction too tight for the tows, at 172 metres overall. Those in France, more recently constructed, are 176 metres long.

At the other extreme, pleasure craft may use a small, totally automatic lock alongside each big one. Just enter the chamber, press a button, and the whole lot works as if by magic. There is a notice in four languages disclaiming responsibility if it does not, but the matter was entirely academic in our case, since the chambers are only 3 metres wide and *Arthur* was 4.30.

Another bemusing characteristic of the Mosel, as on other new waterways, is the lack of safe places to moor. The jetties at locks are usually well out of town, while the average quayside is assailed by wash. It was surprising, all the same, that Trier, the Capital of Roman Gaul, should be so unprovided with places to stop. The barge port is miles away, and the only jetties are jealously guarded by the steamship companies. Short of anchoring there is little alternative but to go alongside a steamer herself and pray that the captain is hospitable. The one I selected proved just so; this was agreeable at first until the crew, who were Dutch, insisted on our joining a lethal game of cards. The first person to lose a point had to choose a drink; the second to pay for it, and the third one to drink it. They were a rumbustious, Rabelesian crowd; I later learned that they too had experienced mooring difficulties, and being infrequent visitors to the river had filched their own place at the pontoon after one of the pukka steamers had left.

The Porta Nigra is the *piece de résistance* of Trier, a great black edifice several storeys high, once the gateway to the Roman Empire. There are, additionally, Roman baths (St Barbara's and the Imperial), an amphitheatre (from which most of the stones were stolen in the eighteenth century), a Cathedral, also dating from the Roman period, three churches, numerous museums and a tenth century market

*Smaller craft generally lie astern of
cargo barges in the large lock
chambers. It is advisable to stay
securely moored until other vessels are
well clear, lest their wash should push
the bow round, or pound it against the
wall. Recessed bollards are arranged
at 15 metre intervals in the lock
walls, set in vertical rows.*

Medieval cranes at Trier

cross. Two medieval cranes stand downriver, looking like
honeypots with spoons projecting. The centre of the town,
which brims with German consumer durables, has its streets
paved over and served by buses trundling through at
walking pace. It is odd that such a glamorous, well cared-for
city should not have a better spot at which to tie up.

From here on, for mile after mile, the river runs through
an emerald gorge lined with the bright green vines and
marked occasionally by wine villages: Trittenheim, Neumagen and Bernkastel. *Arthur*'s mooring in Trittenheim was at
the small landing stage of a steamer company; Neumagen
has a jetty. It was at Neumagen that the discovery of a fourth
century tombstone showing a galley with wine barrels

aboard confirmed Roman usage. Bernkastel has a quay, but
there is a small, sheltered haven at Kues, across the river.
Here I met our friendly Dutch captain again, weaving away
from his ship, having miraculously accomplished the
downstream journey also.

The riverside is neat at Kues, with tidy lawns and a sharp-
edged putting green, made of concrete, with precisely cast
hazards and chicanes. A staggering feature to British eyes
was the presence of a steel lectern, upright, freshly painted
and unmolested, beside each tee. From each lectern there
hung on new clean string a freshly-sharpened pencil. In
France such a complex would have become the refuge of
chickens, and the score, if you wanted to keep it, would be

scratched on the ground with a stick. It might be taking the parallel too far to suggest that the eighteenth hole would be missing.

From Kues a smartly-attired ferryman will take the traveller across the river, as an alternative to Bernkastel Bridge. Bernkastel has half-timbered houses, painted up to the nines, and a reputation for gaiety in early September when the Wine Festival is launched. To complete the film-set picture, a ruined castle, Burg Landshut, looks down from a nearby crag.

The Mosel vines grow from fragmented slate. The slopes are terraced scree, up which the sprayers and pickers must sometimes be winched, so steep is the incline. The grapes

mature through the capacity of the rocks to absorb heat during the day and emit it after nightfall, but to the casual picker they remain sharp and harsh, belying the delicacy of the dry white wine that they produce.

There are more villages along the way, and although Bullay is not one of the most attractive, it was made memorable for me by a powerful steam locomotive, brought to a standstill on the girder bridge. The clatter from the footplate and the numerous hissings and clickings were interrupted by a mournful howling for the signal. Then the firebox door was opened, to let a red shaft of light up into the sky, before the train moved off again, a lumbering snake of iron ore cars gathering speed into the tunnel on the other

Motorway under construction across the Moselle.

Trittenheim, with vineyards in the background. Arthur, moored to one of the steamer stagings, is about to feel the effects of wash from a rare passing pleasure boat.

*Motorway crossing in the lower
reaches, near Koblenz.*

*Construction of Burg Eltz began in the
twelfth century, and the structure has
survived entirely unscathed. The
approach remains by pathway only, a
three or four mile walk from the river
through the forest.*

side. Steam haulage has gone now from the Mosel valley,
and from the rest of Germany too, although it endured until
the mid-1970s, an almost Wagnerian element.

The perfect decking material has yet to be invented, and
the roofing felt that clads *Arthur*, admirable though it is, has
three defects. The first, which need not be taken too
seriously, is that people think it un-nautical and cheap; the
second, which can be very serious, is its capacity for
absorbing the sun in a heatwave. A third is its solubility in
petrol. This we learned while moored at Cochem, where the
long-suffering autocyle, nicknamed initially 'The Power
Chief' but later referred to almost unconsciously as 'Fred',
fell over during the night as the wash of a passing barge
swept us against the quay. The fuel tank emptied onto the
felt, to soak out an irritating tarry substance that several
people trod in. You cannot be too careful at one of these

Moselle moorings, and particularly at the occasional town, where stone or concrete edges reflect the wash. This feature apart, Cochem is another romantic place, topped with the sort of castle that features on posters, and full of cheerful ladies from the Ruhr stepping out arm-in-arm from the beer halls.

Perhaps the most celebrated castle of the region is the medieval Burg Eltz, reached by walking from Karden or Hatzenport. The four mile hike from Karden begins with a scramble through the vineyards before reaching a wide plateau. There follows a long descent into the thickly wooded Eltz valley, and the path through the trees is reminiscent of a Hitchcock thriller of the thirties, with occasional glimpses of the castle as the track winds this way and that. The castle itself, heavily turreted around its paths and courtyards, has survived because the valley in which it stands is off the main highway for brigands and adventurers. It endured only one siege – from the Archbishop of Trier – and the odd skirmish, and remains a private residence, open to lawful visitors. Despite their having to walk, the ladies from the Ruhr find their way here also, and sit in the courtyard saying 'cheers' from behind long tankards of lager.

There are two more castles before Koblenz, Ehrenburg and Thurant; also a towering modern viaduct, no less impressive in its way. Together with one other in the higher reaches, still under construction when we passed, this was the only intrusion of the motorway machine; and so lofty was it that it belonged to another world, literally on a different plane.

Koblenz, once heavily under French influence and a second Paris, was extensively damaged by bombing in 1944. It has been thoroughly reconstructed since. Some early architecture survives, but only the base of a collossal equestrian statue of Kaiser Wilhelm I now remains at Deutsches Eck, the actual confluence with the Rhine. A clamber over its stonework affords a view of the roaring river and of Ehrenbreitstein, the citadel on the other side.

Those in search of a quiet, unjostled mooring are advised to stay in the Moselle overnight. They may lie against the last wall before the junction, on the town side, opposite the spot where the local pusher tugs dump their cargoes. Here the barges are collected into even bigger convoys, ready for the next stage of their journey, down the Rhine.

The Rhine, from Koblenz to Lobith

Downstream is the direction to travel on this wild sweeping river. It is the custom of British politicians, faced with making one of the rare public statements on waterways, to refer to the Rhine as 'a natural highway'. The inference is that Britain's waterways are not, and cannot ever be. Others write their scripts, and can never have been over to look.

The Rhine is both swift and shallow. In the upper reaches there are rocks, and in winter fog and ice. The average speed at Koblenz is four knots, and in the Binger Loch, on the way up to Mainz, it is over six. On occasion these figures double. Despite this there is an impressive traffic up to Switzerland, where the navy is no longer a myth. The first tow of barges reached Basle in 1904, after extensive works in the section above Strasbourg. Further attention has been aimed at increasing the average depth in the higher reaches from the average of 5 ft 5 in, and completion of the chain of locks above Strasbourg has greatly eased the passage. Canalization will ultimately extend the navigation into Lake Constance.

The depths at different points along the river are broadcast every morning in much the same style as the British shipping forecast; but those who start at Koblenz for the journey to the Netherlands will miss the most difficult and spirited section. Nonetheless, some basic requirements should be met: a good chart of the river, obtainable from chandleries along the way; some knowledge of the signalling system between barges, or 'ships' as they are often known; and the right combination of prudence and concentration. A multitude of flag signals are deployed, but

The days of Rhine towing, recorded in the narrows near Bingen with one of the last paddle tugs (page 24), designed to overcome currents in excess of eight knots. The upstream passage from the Ruhr to Mannheim might take eight days, with the tow divided for the most rapid section of the river, and the tug making a double journey, with two large barges in each tow. (Raab Karcher GmbH)

Traffic on the Rhine, seen from the Drachenfels. (previous page)

The Ruhr (below)

the basic one, as on French rivers, is the blue flag or board. This is often displayed on the starboard side of the wheelhouse of a vessel hammering upstream, revealing her skipper's intention to pass an oncoming vessel on the 'wrong' side, that is to say 'starboard side to', or in English canal parlance, 'keeping to the left'. Downcomers hoist a similar blue signal to acknowledge.

It is tempting to suggest that small craft should merely keep out of the way, but they will be hard put to do so in certain cases and must willy-nilly join the system. At one point, Remagen, near the remnants of the bridge that the American Army crossed in 1945, *Arthur* was overtaken by four barges simultaneously. At the same time I counted sixteen upcomers between ourselves and the next bend, one of which, a 1,000-tonner from the Dortmund-Ems Canal pushing a similar vessel in tandem, had plainly become tired of being stationary in the stream and was sidling across to try her luck near the other bank. In the bottleneck there

she appeared to be straddling most of the main channel.

Our first experience of entering the river at Koblenz was that the traffic was evenly divided between those who were blue-flagging and those who were not. Thus we passed directly between the two philosophies, bobbing like a cork in the turmoil. Our own blue flag was frequently deployed, and since it tended to stream horizontally in the wind, we had to tie down its corners. This is why sophisticates use a board, operated by a button or cord from the comfort of a wheelhouse. At night a flashing light is substituted, but that is the time for the sane visitor to be lurking in a haven.

These can be difficult to find. Due to a misunderstanding of Roger Pilkington's otherwise excellent *Waterways in Europe*, I confused left bank with right; so we moored in all manner of interesting places: a swamp-like backwater at Honnef and a rock-lined coal harbour at Cologne. In both cases there are said to be better hideaways on the west bank. We moored on the east.

Getting into these moorings involves a broadside, sliding turn, passing close to the stone groynes that project at regular intervals and the bobbing buoys that mark the shingle edge between them. A further interesting obstruction is provided by the occasional eel-fishing boat, permanently tethered to support a funnel-shaped ground net on a projecting spar. The eels remain tasty, despite the pollution of the lower river, since they do not feed here. The craft themselves are often handsome sailing vessels, Dutch in origin.

Bad Honnef has lovely old trams, and an *Emil and the Detectives* journey takes one to Königswinter, thence by rack-railway to the summit of the Drachenfels. The Valkyries lived here, replaced today by elegant German waiters dispensing beer at extortionate prices; but the view is terrific, of the Rhine traffic, of Bonn, and of the place one should have moored. The *Drachen* itself was slain by Siegfried, who bathed in its blood; the conical mountain, made more so by quarrying, is the northern outpost of

German viniculture. Those who relish wine, and have become accustomed to its easy purchase, are advised to buy some, as prices in Holland may come as a shock.

Bonn has no obvious moorings, but Cologne has the welcoming Rheinauhafen on the west side, and the grim but secure industrial basin on the east. On a lowering day the tough Germanic aspect of this rebuilt city is in no way softened by the hideous stink in the reaches just below. An outfall here was turning the river bright purple when *Arthur* passed; a lashing cross-wind, flurries of rain, and the ever-pounding river traffic confirmed the inhospitable nature of the main stream. Should your vessel break down, there is no sensible place to lie. Big lignite transporter barges are to be seen moored against the strewn rocks that line the river bank, but anything of lesser stature will graunch horribly in the wash. There is no option for those who have had enough and wish to fight another day but to turn into a scrofulous backwater at Hitdorf. This was thick with decayed chemistry when *Arthur* called.

The passage of Düsselforf is marked by elegant bridges, one of which, a suspension span, was recently moved several yards to one side to conform with a realignment of roads. Düsseldorf is a slick, modern city with skyscrapers and, almost unnoticed, a remnant of castle by the riverside. There are yacht moorings in the main stream and commercial basins on the east, or more correctly southern bank, for the river makes another snaking loop just before the main town.

Some 25 kilometres further downstream comes the Ruhr, a witches' cauldron of heavy industry. Much of it is sited up the Rhine-Herne Canal, which branches off at Duisburg. Many large barges muster at this point, among them the bigger push-tows, which tower above the other traffic. The docks of Duisburg, Ruhrort and Meiderich occupy an area three times that of Liverpool and Birkenhead in their heyday, and conducted tours by boat are available. A further feature of the area is the way in which the Rhine has dropped eight feet since the turn of the century, through the natural action of the current, and the Duisburg basins are kept on the same level by means of coal-mining underneath.

The Rhine-Herne Canal connects through an area of smoke and clamour, and via numerous locks, with the Dortmund-Ems Canal. From this it is possible to reach the Weser, the Elbe and a large part of East Germany, by means of linking waterways. There are ghoulish stories of barges straying the wrong side of the frontier line on the Elbe and being machine-gunned, and a large new canal has recently been opened to bypass the loop and reduce these incidents. East German and Polish barges are often seen on the Rhine, however; wan grey things whose occupants gaze fixedly at craft like *Arthur*. These vessels bear no names, only numbers, and I wondered what they made of the highly individualistic craft called *Nelly* and so forth, chugging this way and that, so plainly their own masters.

There is another link with the German canal system at Wesel, where there is also a marina. Those who are

A paddle-drawn tow, sweeping wide on a shallow bend. Despite their size and power, the tugs had a draught of 1.05 metres only. (Raab Karcher GmbH)

impressed by the standard of watermanship among the barge community may draw consolation from the shambles that can prevail in a German pleasure boat harbour. Superstitious as I am in criticising nautical mishaps, it was difficult to restrain a self-righteous glee at the demonstrations of human frailty. Ropes were tossed into the air, and into the water, grannys and slip-knots were tied, vessels rammed quays and others went aground. All this, despite the enforcement of Certificates of Competence for German nationals on the Rhine.

We helped drag a sailing cruiser off a hidden reef and took her out into the main stream, where I expected her to spend the rest of the day beating ineffectually into the current. On the contrary, she set off like a bullet downstream, with all sails hoisted and sheets freed for a brisk run before the wind. This is a common habit in Rhine yachting; and at the end of the day a sailing boat will hang about in the main channel, until a friendly barge thunders up and offers a tow back to base. This is a hair-raising procedure, as the natural speed at which most craft can travel is related to their size. The square root of twice the waterline length in feet, yields the maximum speed possible, expressed in knots. Thus a barge travelling at twelve knots may be towing a small boat with a theoretical maximum of perhaps seven knots only. There are two ways out: either the smaller craft disintegrates, which is what usually happens when yachts are taken in tow at sea; or she 'planes', rising part way out of the water. On boats not especially designed for planing, the effect is nerve-racking. And yet displacement sailing craft are often dragged back up the Rhine in this manner, shuddering on the crest of the wake, their occupants sitting tight in the cockpit with their lifejackets on.

Rarely now, a chain of towed barges may be encountered, working in the old style, with the tug leading. By custom each dumb barge is pulled on a separate line, despite being arranged in single file, and there are elaborate techniques for hitching up a tow, grappling up the cables from the river bed and holding them side by side along each intermediate barge. In the old days the lines of barges would be astern of a monster paddle tug, with raked funnels and, because of her shallow draught, the boilers clearly visible on deck. These were monstrous dramatic vessels, thumping like warlords in their struggle against the current. Now, with pushing all the rage, such convoys have become a rarity and the paddle tugs themselves were withdrawn by 1970.

The river keeps its speed all the way to the Dutch frontier at Lobith, an unimpressive place with only a small haven to draw into. The pusher tows and motor barges round up in midstream, their crews scampering around the anchor winches; and because of the confusion this creates there are separate clearance ports for the different directions. Upcomers clear at Emmerich a few kilometres back upstream. The odd determined vessel rushes right through, but unless under Customs bond, with green flags to declare it, she will be waved in by one of the fussing patrol vessels.

Once ashore there are corridors to plod through and offices to visit. The German one is obsessed with fuel forms. If you have kept a record, as specified, a rebate may be claimed on taxation paid on fuel. Figures must be applied on tankage on entering and on leaving the country, and great is the bafflement if the latter exceeds the former, through having refuelled in Luxembourg. With another bureaucratic assault in prospect, it seemed a good idea to realize that a mistake had been made, and to adjust the figures. The Customs man was very relieved when I did this, and after indicating the forms we had avoided filling, went on to tell me about his holidays in Canada. I suspect we lost on the deal, but just could not get my mind around what was going on.

The Dutch Customs were rather like those of Luxembourg and not terribly interested, but suspecting that it might be a good idea, I got a piece of paper from them recognizing our entry into the Netherlands. In the whole of the two years that followed in the country, I was never asked to produce this certificate again.

The Netherlands – Introduction

The Dutch are an uncantankerous race, who cheerfully print 'Holland' all over their tourist literature, in deference to British tastes. Correctly speaking, North Holland and South Holland are but two of the original eleven provinces of the country, to which a twelfth is now being added with the draining of the Zuyder Zee. 'The Netherlands', itself an anglicization, is the more correct title. 'Nederland' is the one the people use themselves.

It is not a big country, but it has all manner of difficulties, being by nature an uneasy swamp. From this the Dutch people, with their characteristic industriousness, have fashioned a land that is both pleasant and welcoming. It is also barge country, and in the following pages I have dwelt a little on the lore of these vessels, as well as on my own experiences in buying one, *Secunda*, successor to *Arthur*. None of this need deter those in smaller craft. Having visited several areas in yachts myself, I have drawn on those voyages also; and in dealing with the Dutch waterways, section by section, I have combined these experiences to be of greater practical value to those who may wish to follow.

Dordrecht

1	IJsselmeer	25	R. Eem
2	van Harinxma Canal	26	Hollandsche IJssel
3	Prinses Margriet Canal	27	R. Vecht
4	Starkenborgh Canal	28	Amsterdam-Rhine Canal
5	Opsterlandsche Compagnonsvaart	29	Westeinder Plassen
6	Tjonger Canal	30	R. Amstel
7	Meppeler Diep	31	North Sea Canal
8	IJssel	32	North Holland Canal
9	Neder Rijn	33	Volkerak
10	R. Lek	34	Krammer
11	R. Rhine	35	Haringvliet
12	Rhine-Herne Canal	36	Spui
13	Zuid Willemsvaart	37	Grevelingen
14	R. Maas	38	Zijpe
15	R. Waal	39	Ooster Schelde
16	Beneden Merwede	40	Wester Schelde
17	Wantij	41	Albert Canal
18	Biesbos	42	Gent Ship Canal
19	Nieuwe Merwede	43	C. de Plasschendale (sic)
20	Hollandsch Diep	44	C. de Furnes
21	Dordtsche Kil	45	C. de Bourbourg
22	Noord Canal	46	La Liason Dunkerque-Valenciennes
23	Ketelmeer	47	R. Aa
24	Zwartemeer	48	C. de Calais

Lobith to Dordrecht – the Waal

The Rhine, a muscular bully for much of its course, fizzles out in its later reaches. Not far beyond the German border the river splits, and its several branches acquire many names. The Oude Rijn, as the Dutch term it, is a watercourse of little consequence, reappearing from out of the tangle somewhere near Utrecht, and from there it wobbles off towards the sea. From the German border onwards the foremost route is the Waal. In its early stages it can still run swiftly, the traffic continues to be dense, and there are lethal groynes that project out into the stream. They are marked by buoys or posts and it is said that the shrewd traveller can exploit the eddies their ends create, but too fine a judgement is needed from ordinary mortals.

There are several tight bends. On the outside of one is the Waalhaven, the smaller but more welcoming port at Nijmegen. The current whistles across its entrance, and through a navigational miscalculation *Arthur* pranged the wall here, though little harm was done. Inside, a rectangular basin provides a home for slumbering cargo craft, many of them small barges pensioned off as houseboats. Nearby may be found a real Dutch rarity, a hill, at the top of which a vigorous market affords the opportunity of eating smoked fish and glimpsing the river and its traffic through gaps between the stalls. Much knocked about in the war, Nijmegen has its share of replacement architecture, but some older parts remain, cheerful and intimate in scale. As everywhere in Holland there is a predeliction for antiques, both real and imaginary; I was staggered to see for sale a

British grill pan, *circa* 1960 and in need of a good wash.

Downstream the countryside flattens, the current lessens. Wide, swirling skies take over, and it needs a mental wrench to recall the wooded hillsides and pastureland of France. As the drubbing of diesels continues unabated it remains

Warehouses at Zwijndrecht, bearing the names of former Dutch colonies.

important to find a haven, and thanks to the excellent *waterkaarten*, referred to later, these are easily spotted. There is a good harbour at Zaltbommel, a sheltered pool overlooked by a windswept row of houses, stuck up on the flood wall. Thousand-ton barges unload here, but there is space at the back, tended by an amiable harbourmaster who invites all yachtsmen to sign his visitors book.

Gradually, as the current decreases, it begins to dawn on the downstream traveller that the river has become vaguely tidal, and by the time Gorinchem is reached it is possible to see marker buoys set the other way by the incoming current. Gorinchem, where two canals branch off to the north, is an almost impossible place to ask for. Mention 'Goring-chem' and few will understand, even among the many Netherlanders who speak good English. The Dutch pronunciation is 'Horror-come', or something rather like it.

Across the main river a portion of the Maas enters, another river with many divisions, and rather a doleful one, lacking the grandeur of its upper reaches in Belgium and in France. The Maas is a busy trade route, despite its tendency to flooding. There can be long queues of barges at its locks, which have increased in number through the years as the Dutch have indulged their passion for construction projects. Those venturing up the Maas may expect long waits; likewise in the Zuid Willemsvaart, a canal apparently drawn on the map with a ruler, to cut across the river's big sweeping loop through southeast Holland. The high spots of the Maas are Maastricht itself, 'the oldest town in Holland'; Maasbracht, one of those places at which it is alleged that good cheap barges are for sale (and which, upon being visited, proves entirely empty of them); and on the connecting canals, s'Hertogenbosch, with its celebrated marketplace and cathedral, and Breda, where the castle and several Gothic churches survive amidst the industry.

These connections add to the traffic on the Waal, which near Gorinchem changes its name again and becomes the Boven Merwede. Other junctions and diversions follow; the

Upper doorway by the Wolwevershaven

meadows give way to continuous wharves; the water is thrashed by pulsating traffic. By the time Dordrecht is reached, on what has become the Beneden Merwede, the traveller in any small vessel is rushing about sweeping up crockery and securing loose furniture.

Despite the hubbub, Dordrecht has numerous sheltered basins. A marina may be entered, near the leaning tower of the Grote Kerk, and there are sundry commercial harbours opposite the entrance to the Noord Canal, the wide main route to Rotterdam. Entry to these havens is under little metal drawbridges, operated at all manner of odd hours including, in my own observation, after midnight on a Sunday morning, by a perky figure arriving on a bike. Local enquiry is suggested, although the bridges are high enough to let many yachts through without opening. If obliged to wait outside it is better to do so alongside a moored barge some distance away, since there are cranky corners to several of the basins, in which the wash from the main waterway ricochets and slaps.

Despite these difficulties, loaded sand barges manage to enter the Wolwevershaven stern first, which they prefer to do in view of the limited turning space inside. The basin itself is surrounded by delightful buildings and enticing trees, but the overhanging ones should be avoided as they become laden with starlings at dusk. The citizens have a long-standing vendetta against the birds, and frequently ignite thunderflashes to disturb them. These certainly surprise the visitors.

There are pleasant alleys for an evening stroll, however, and characterful displays of broken anchors and torn propellers. These are left casually on the pavement near a repair yard with a hoist for 350-ton barges, which in Holland are known as *spits*. In the next basin, the marina, stands the van Gijn Museum, an elegant town house furnished in the styles of different periods.

Overriding all is the thud of passing barge traffic. Just across the Wolwevershaven a gap in the housing leads to a *winkelschip*, a floating supermarket, the largest in Europe, where barge crews can choose their washing machines and tape recorders, as well as the tools of their trade.

At the far side of the great river is Zwijndrecht, with a line of warehouses bearing names from the old colonial days: Java, Rangoon and Siam; and still today, as the voyager bounces by, there are smells of hardwood and spices borne across the water.

Waterkaarten and Bridges

Bridge and counterbalance at Dordecht

For those intent on lingering in the Netherlands there is a bewildering maze to choose from. So complex is the Dutch water system that good maps are vital, and they come no better than the *Waterkaarten*, published by the ANWB, the Royal Dutch Touring Club. They may be bought at shops in every major town. Some sixteen maps cover the bulk of the system, each to a large scale with elaborate symbols and colour coding. Waters shown in blue are available to motor boats. Depths are given, and so are bridge clearances, all in decimetres, e.g. D25 – meaning depth 2.5 metres, W70 – width 7 metres, H5 – height 0.5 metres, and so on. Overhead clearance is generally the critical dimension and it helps to know the height of one's boat. The expression BB, printed upon the map, means an opening bridge. Think of Brigitte Bardot, I once was told (some time ago, when that lady seemed to wink from every magazine); and thus distracted I went up a waterway where all the bridges were BB except the last. It is important to check a route all the way through, since small waterways sometimes peter out.

Those who have tussled with English lift and swing bridges, seeking out crowbars and jacking equipment while engaging in fisticuffs with impatient motorists, will be pleasantly surprised by the Dutch approach. Several British waterways cannot be restored because of lowered roadways, and any proposal to interrupt motor traffic will give the County Surveyor *delirium tremens*. The Dutch simply put a movable bridge in. They have thousands of them, ranging from tiny neo-oriental structures wound by handles, to steel and reinforced concrete gantries. There are even bridges on motorways, protected by banks of traffic lights, and each one has a keeper. Occasionally, on a little-used route or in the narrow old canals at the centre of a town, the keeper must be winkled out of a nearby house, or from the cabin of the next bridge along if he works two. But generally there is a man already on duty, acknowledging one's approach by changing the warning lights to a combination of red and green, and then to green as he presses a button and the span lifts. On some of the older waterways, and more particularly in Friesland in the north, a clog is swung out on a fishing rod as the vessel passes, in anticipation of a small coin. Until recently a 25 cent *kwartje* would suffice, but with inflation half a guilder, just over ten pence, is now more appropriate.

In planning a route it must be born in mind that bridges in the centre of towns often work at certain hours only, usually as notified in the cabin windows, while some, particularly in the north, are inoperable on Sundays. Concessions have now been made in popular yachting areas, and limited Sunday opening has been introduced in summer. The greatest holdups occur at railway bridges, which naturally have to fit in with the trains. On exceptionally busy lines these bridges open rarely, and sometimes at awkward hours.

It is worth measuring the clearance of any vessel percisely, perhaps using a length of string or a pole while up some minor canal. I did this on *Arthur* several times, to check heights with tanks both full and empty. My usual method is to station the boat beneath a bridge, having measured the distance of the arch above water. Deducting the clearance above the highest point of the boat then gives the height of the boat above water.

In approaching any bridge it must be remembered that water levels may vary, and that even the *waterkaart* cannot always be precise. A flagstaff on the bow, adjusted to give the correct clearance, is a useful form of warning. The *péniche* technique is to have a long mast canted back at an angle, and set, according to load and trim, by means of a pulley system at the base. The mast is raised to the height of the cabin roof and if it can pass beneath a bridge without upsetting the masthead lamp, which is set in a pivot, the wheelhouse will pass under also.

The bridge-keeper receives his tip, by clog suspended from a pole. (Hugh Potter)

The Wantij, the Biesbos, and Ducks

Off the main routes are many byways. It is one of the delights of the Dutch system that small intricate waterways can lie so close to broad, bustling ones. Such a canal is the Wantij, which tucks around the back of Dordrecht.

Its entrance is cluttered with shipyards, but gradually it becomes *Arthur*-sized. A lift-bridge and a modern highway cross it, but then, a mile or so beyond, follow scenes from the Middle Ages: a shack-like homestead with milk churns, raving geese and a pig. Shortly afterwards, around a tight little turn, is a hexagonal lock, lined with old wooden stagings at which a boat may safely lie while the keeper gently operates the gates and sluices. It was here that I encountered the most egocentric bird in the world, a white duck. It could be heard five minutes before it came, its shrill weck-wecking so insistent that I thought there was something the matter with the engine. It entered the lock with us, then attempted to drill a hole in the hull by machine-like pecking. Through sheer force of character this bird extracted several slices of bread from us, before executing a vertical takeoff and disappearing, still making a din.

Ducks are the minor tyrants of the Dutch waterways. Bloated and overfed, they stagger up and down the quaysides. Holland is said to be a nation of dogs and cats; indeed furry, pudding-like lumps may be glimpsed through practically every window, sleeping off the latest feast, but the ducks run them pretty close. In some canals people put out special raffia nests for them, loaded with porcelain eggs to encourage them to lay. There the ducks hold committee meetings, day and night, especially at night.

These are town ducks, villains and hooligans, but gentler, wilder species also reside in the Netherlands. A good place to see them is in the Biesbos, a wild marshy area also close to Dordrecht. It is reached by passing through the Wantij and the little lock I have described, and crossing the Nieuwe Merwede, another big river outside. A further lock on the opposite shore gives access to this region of shallow lakes and islands. The Biesbos is Arthur Ransome country, an area of twisting streams and jungly backwaters, occupying some twenty-five square miles. It was created by the St Elizabeth's flood of 1421, when thousands died as the dykes collapsed and formed the big estuary nearby, the Hollandsch Diep. Until recently all this area was strongly tidal, but the coastal defence works of the south have rendered it less so, and scarcely any change in level occurs at all.

It is a region of surprises. We found a small bohemian community residing in a string of Ark-like houseboats up one of the backwaters, and ran so fiercely aground in another of the streams that it took an hour of working *Arthur* to and fro, using tiller and engine, to free her from the silt. In the evenings we would moor with a view across a wider expanse, to watch the cormorants and grebes.

The giant Peruvian boyfriend of one of my crew was induced to leap ashore at one point, to moor us at a time of crisis before we were blown off the bank of an uninhabited island. I found him later, sitting with his feet in a bucket of water, having trampled, in response to urgent instructions, through dense beds of nettles. His feet had been unshod, a common warm-weather affectation on boats which usually leads to injury of some kind. I have sailed with people whose feet became balls of sticking plaster through the constant collision with cleats and anchor. On inland waterways the hazards come when leaping ashore: spiky gravel at towns, thorns and stinging things in regions like the Biesbos.

By a variety of routes, it is possible to return quickly

to the hustle of Dordrecht. For the best in contrasts, it is stimulating, and if the wind is fresh quite wit-sharpening, to make for the southwest corner of the Biesbos and out into the Hollandsch Diep. Here sizeable rollers smash against the bow, and although by seagoing standards their effect is tame, it is a salutary reminder of the discomforts and apprehensions of deep-water sailing. A big railway viaduct

crosses the water here, with a road bridge alongside it, so it is not really a sea at all; after the Biesbos it merely seems like it.

Just beyond the bridges a busy commerical waterway, the Dordsche Kil, leads directly back to Dordrecht, where the giant pusher tugs wait for the main lift bridge to open, and the day when a new road tunnel will replace it.

Minor tyrants of the waterways: ducks congregate by the waterside in a town canal.

Exploring the stream between two of the many islands in the Biesbos, once a tidal marsh. (left)

Fog, the Noord Canal and Rotterdam

The Noord connects Dordecht and a point near Rotterdam. These are normal traffic conditions.

skippers of large craft switch on their radar sets and gallop along as before. It is quite an experience to have 2,000 tons from Antwerp appearing from behind your left ear. A substantial tonnage proceeds in this manner, and the mass of converging traffic is augmented by the ferries, which are numerous in Holland, flitting to and fro between the conflicting fleets. To be seen is not enough. Every skipper has to read the situation, and take avoiding action early.

Caught in fog in *Arthur*, the obvious course was to make towards the bank. Two smaller motor barges in the process of overtaking when the first mist descended promptly did this, their captains cutting down speed to a crawl, and sending people forward to look and listen. It is important to make for the bank on the starboard-hand side; one consolation of fog is that the nuances of blue-flagging are abandoned and the basic rule of the road adhered to.

The fringes of the Noord are largely industrial, a litter of wharves and inlets. The local *waterkaart, Grote Rivieren – Middenblad*, is valuable in providing warning of sundry jetties. Most particularly, it shows the junction with the Lek, another of the Great Rivers, as the Rhine's several offspring are known. To saunter out into the confluence, unbeknownst, must be one of life's more disorienting experiences, particularly as there are several backwaters on the farther bank to confuse the arrival. In the thickest fog the obvious course is to stop moving altogether and the simplest mooring will be alongside one of the many tethered barges. But my own memories of the area are happy ones: of

There is a lot of fog on Dutch inland waterways, particularly in the early morning. On the narrow canals of France it is the custom to send some aged relative up to the bow of a barge, to peer anxiously ahead while the vessel blunders forward. On big Dutch waterways, such as the Noord Canal, the

the fog lifting sufficiently to reveal a ferry crossing the Lek, silhouetted like a sampan against the mist, while a large sea-going tanker stood high in drydock on the bank, reflecting in her oxidised sides the first of the morning sun.

The great port complex of Rotterdam lies mainly on the seaward side of the city, a maze of industry and activity. The New Waterway, Nieuwe Waterweg, linking Rotterdam with the sea was opened in 1872. It has thereafter prospered, save during World War II, when it was largely destroyed. But even then, under German occupation, plans for its extension were hatched in secret. Scheme has followed scheme, and all have been carried out. With the creation of a new port on the Maas Sands, beyond the Hook of Holland entrance, the expansion has now moved out to sea. There is an exhibition centre in the midst, the Eur-o-rama, which lies directly opposite the ferry terminal at the Hook of Holland, and a tripping boat plies in summer.

Rotterdam itself is a glassy commercial city, encircled by highways. At night the many blocks of flats are uniformly lit by the blue glow of television, it being a Dutch habit not to pull curtains. 'If we saw a house with the curtains drawn', I have been told, 'we would say, hello, what is going on in there?' It is a law-abiding place. When a Dutch friend left his camera clearly visible in the back of his car he thought it odd when I suggested that it might be stolen. And it was difficult to know where to look after a squad of British football fans had tried to smash up the place. The citizens were genuinely bemused.

The visitor arriving by boat may head for sundry commercial basins, assuming he does not mind the light

being blocked out when some slab-sided monster moors alongside him. The majority head instead for the KR & ZV de Maas, the Royal Yacht Club of the Maas, an oasis of calm and considerate hospitality. Its headquarters are in the first harbour on the northern bank upstream of the Euromast, an observation point 117 metres high affording a splendid view of the port complex.

Push-tow at Spijkenisse, near Rotterdam

Routes to Amsterdam

From Rotterdam, there are several alternatives. Though they traverse a part of the country severely affected by motorwayitis, none is objectionable. Frequently on embankments, since the land around has subsided through enthusiastic drainage, they afford views of windmills, glasshouses and a degree of cultivated country in between. They are calmer in atmosphere than the bustling Great Rivers, so good places to lie are less difficult to find.

The westernmost course is entered through the Park Locks (Parksluizen) in the centre of Rotterdam, and proceeds by Delft, Leiden and, if desired, Harlem, although an alternative and more direct route is through the Westeinder Plassen, biggest of a group of lakes used extensively by sailing craft in summer. Aalsmeer, on the Westeinder Plassen, is the site of the largest flower auction in the world.

Delft is beautiful at its centre, with a most imposing square, while a pottery still survives; but its outskirts resemble some exhibit from the Leggo toy brick factory, and there is nowhere really pleasant to lie. Having trudged the streets of The Hague in search of a tax office, I am similarly prejudiced against that, and since only the smallest boats can make towards it from nearby Rijswijk, it is not worth getting stuck under a bridge for. Leiden has much more to offer, being the oldest university town in the country, and correspondingly attractive. Among its museums is one devoted to windmills, which fall into many types, featured *ad infinitum* on postcards and matchbox labels. Haarlem, similarly, has a delightful centre, with its famous church of St Bavo and staggering organ, installed in 1738, while those in pursuit of bulbfields will find them on the route from Leiden. The best time to visit is in April, and there is a demonstration garden at Hillegom.

The canal between Leiden and Haarlem is also part of a ring surrounding the Haarlemmermeer Polder. This was once another big lake, rough enough for ships to seek shelter in a specially constructed harbour at Schipol, where the airport now stands. After many a scheme, it was finally drained in the mid-nineteenth century, with steam pumps.

A more attractive route is that to Gouda, and thence directly to Amsterdam. It is the only one remaining for yachts with fixed masts, provided their crews do not mind waiting until after midnight to get through the railway bridge by Amsterdam's main station; but the most varied and interesting route of all in my estimation is that passing up the Hollandsche IJssel, beyond Gouda, as described in the next chapter, and down the lovely River Vecht.

Tidal Charts and the Hollandsche IJssel

At Krimpen, the voyager from Dordrecht, now something of a rough water dog, may turn away before reaching Rotterdam and its even greater tumult, to make his escape up the Hollandsche IJssel. This is a river with a double gateway at its mouth, two 260 ft spans worthy of the Pharaohs. After the 1953 disaster, the government, provoked by the disastrous flooding from the sea, set in motion the Delta Plan. The Krimpen gates were an early construction. At times of dangerously high tides they are lowered, a rare but necessary event. With typical Dutch emphasis on continuing navigation, a lock has been built alongside, even though, for 999 days out of a thousand, it is possible to sail directly under these huge storm doors.

At first the river is industrial, its shores devoted to shipbuilding. Bulbous bows and the ends of propellers tower above the visiting holidaymaker, and since the water is still strongly tidal there are grids for barges to dry out on. It greatly eases progress if one ascends on the incoming current. By good fortune *Arthur* did so, although later experience in this area was not so happy, and I spent much time heading into streams I would rather have known about in advance.

By the time Gouda is reached, the river has dwindled. There is a turnoff before the town to the direct route to Amsterdam, and in here are the better moorings. As so often nowadays, the oldest, tiny canals of the town centre have low fixed bridges, which limit their use to dinghies. For those continuing up the Hollandsche IJssel there is a noisy, dusty mooring beside the main road. From here it is but a short step to the main square, well worth visiting for the Gothic town hall, a splendidly ornate affair, with red and white quartered shutters. Photographs of it are a little flattering, since there is a maddening clutter of lampposts and railings, but it is pleasant indeed to sit in a café on the fringe and gaze across at this spikily ornamented pile. In the St Janskerk nearby, the largest church in the Netherlands,

Storm doors for flood prevention at Krimpen, on the Hollandsche IJssel.

are sixty-four stained-glass windows, fourteen of them dating from the sixteenth century. On the way to it are numerous pleasant shops with tiled interiors, while on my own visit there was also an immaculately preserved travelling organ, a superb piece of folk art albeit powered by electric motor, with mechanical drummer and tympanist. Not only were passers-by contributing coins, but the operator was knocking on house doors, brandishing a polished brass collecting can. No-one seemed to begrudge a contribution.

The real transformation in the Hollandsche IJssel occurs at the Waiierschutsluis. At 26 metres overall this is a short lock, but a complex one. It stands just outside the town, with double sets of gates, to resist tidal pressure when the rise exceeds the level of water beyond. Amiable keepers work the gear.

The odd small barge passes through, but from here onwards the waterway, now a canal in character, resembles the English Trent & Mersey as it potters across green meadows. Its course includes the village of Oudewater (witches' scales from 1595, cheese production, a stork's nest on the rooftops), Montfoort (medieval, among modern semi-detached) and IJsselstein (a sixteen century castle). There are sundry small wharves, some visited by barges little larger than *Arthur*, in full working trim. While it was a treat to tie to the bank and watch the passing of a small sand barge of some 80 tons capacity, it was less amusing to run down the bank in pursuit of *Arthur* when the mooring pins pulled away. Wherever traffic passes, of any size, it is vital to tie to something solid. For a vessel of *Arthur*'s weight, iron bollards are preferred, failing that solid fenceposts or a suitable tree. The towpath, a prominent feature of the French canals, is a rarity in the Netherlands. The path tends to be a muddy cow track along the top of a dyke, often quite distant from the water. As a result the whirring autocyclist and pre-dawn angler, so often to be found suspended from mooring lines or lying semi-concious on the waterside paths of France, are not a feature here. On the other hand, strong points are often absent also.

Towards the end of its wriggling course, the Hollandsche IJssel is joined by a long straight canal. Two more locks, one rustic, one vast, release the traveller into modernity once again, the Amsterdam–Rhine Canal.

A travelling organ, seen at Gouda

Gouda town hall

The Amsterdam–Rhine Canal

This is the quick way from Amsterdam to the Waal, a wide, busy route with concrete edges that reflect and perpetuate the wash of each passing monster. Opened in 1952, it is of the motorway era, taking the directest course. It swings out of the dockland warehouses east of Amsterdam and then cuts in long straights to the southeast. High arched bridges cross it from time to time, and there are rows of poplars, but it is too wide to be friendly and anything less than a 1,350 tonner of the standard 'Europe' size looks rather lost on its expanses.

Towards the southern end there are traffic lights, at the crossing of the River Lek. Fixed yellow and flashing bulbs are set in various combinations against black boards. Their message is quite simple: should any one of them be lighted, then something is coming, almost certainly a barge of size and momentum. Pleasure craft must slow down and stay clear. They have no 'rights', 'yachts' being required to keep out of the way of working craft throughout the Netherlands.

There are mooring places along the length of the Amsterdam–Rhine Canal, with bollards provided, under the eye of looming blocks of flats. There is little chance of vandalism, but only those under heavy sedation, or with boats made of India-rubber, will wish to lie here.

The best moorings are down some side canal, of which there are several. Some lead into the labyrinth running through the centre of Utrecht. There the water lies in deep cuttings, with views into spruced-up cellars, pierced under the city streets. This route is for small craft with sleek, streamlined structures, since there are many arched bridges,

Small canals remain navigable in the centre of Utrecht. (Hugh Potter)

A tradesman's mark on the side of a cellar, seen from the canal in Utrecht. (Hugh Potter)

some on bends. Attractive though Utrecht is, I found these canals claustrophobic and preferred the other escape routes into the placid River Vecht.

There is one final obstacle, a subtle one. In several of these cross-cuts the bridges are fixed and their clearances modest. Linger beneath one and the wash of a passing vessel on the main canal may cause a wheelhouse or awning to rise and smite the arch. On the first cut north of Utrecht, there is a lock, sometimes open at both ends, sometimes not, which compels a delay. The wait is better spent rolling out in the main stream than directly beneath the bridge at the entrance.

The Amsterdam–Rhine Canal is a straight busy waterway which is rarely still. (Hugh Potter)

River Vecht

The Vecht is a waterway of style, intricate and twisty. Atmospheric mansions line its banks, with numerous summerhouses among the willow trees and an elegant castle at Nijenrode, upstream of Breukelen. In all the small towns there are lift-bridges. Discreet hooting is required at several, and as there is a slight stream running it is often necessary to tie to the wooden fendering before each span. A good supply of small coins must be laid in for the passage, for this is a wooden clog waterway, on which many but not all of the bridges require a token fee.

Breukelen gave its name to Brooklyn, New York. The Dutch original remains calm, with a handsome centre. At its farther side the Amsterdam–Rhine Canal runs by. There are numerous connections, some of them big enough to receive substantial barges, but few penetrate the Vecht nowadays. In several of the smaller cuts miniature locks may also be glimpsed. Through these it is possible to reach the Loosdrechtse Plassen, a complex of lakes and islands seething with holidaymakers in high summer. More remote moorings can be found in various gravel pits further down.

An anchor is a necessity in Holland, preferably of a type that is suited to silt. The Dutch prefer a twin-bladed kind akin to the Danforth. The CQR plough anchor carried on *Arthur* tended to drag some way before biting; but it permitted us to lie at the centre of a beautiful pool, its edges surrounded by reeds and bulrushes, its surface glassy in the shining dawn. Penetrating a backwater in a dinghy, I discovered a group of old craft left to decay. A brutish tug lay among them, once no doubt a force to be reckoned with on the rapids of the Rhine. Now, bright orange with rust, it lay tilted in the shallows, weeds growing on its decks.

A distinctive feature of the Dutch waterways is the variety of houseboats. In the crowded area south of Amsterdam there are many of them. A few are in shanty communities, but the majority are smart, comfortable craft, maintained in the manner of Dutch houses, meticulously. Potted plants grow in their windows, lamps glow within. On the Vecht there are some proud houseboats indeed. Several are literally houses upon boats, with gables, balconies and thatched roofs. Some are simply-converted motor barges, or comfortable yachts, which can take their owners away to the outer islands or to the Baltic at holiday time.

I have had the good fortune to stay in a houseboat community on one of the backwaters of the Vecht, living with some friends for a short period aboard a steel *tjalk*, a traditional bluff-bowed sailing vessel. The owner ran a shop in Amsterdam; the man on the next boat worked for Hilversum Radio. Others were secretaries or laboratory assistants. How agreeable to return from work in a crowded city to a romantic mooring under trees, with a view across meadows or down among the reeds, with a welcoming ship's stove and a bloated cat. Living in a sizeable well-found craft provides an excellent combination of security and independence. And there is always the feeling that one day, again, the vessel might move on. Our own *tjalk* had travelled over much of Holland in the holidays; it added to the atmosphere on board. She was a ship as well as a house.

At Weesp there is a further lift bridge. Here *Arthur*, after

Houseboats are numerous and various. (Hugh Potter)

Summerhouse on the River Vecht. (right)

much hooting on the battered cornet that we used, was compelled to moor to the staging and wait. The delay was caused by the keeper having to work another bridge as well, up the Smal Weesp. This is a useful side canal, running right through the town and ultimately, under a variety of names, to join the River Amstel at the ramparts of Amsterdam. In its later stages this cross-link is an uninspiring route, lying close to main roads and some horrid suburbs; but the section in Weesp is jolly, even if one has to tie to the public urinal on the quay.

Those continuing down the Vecht need a height of less than four metres above the water for clearance, since the railway bridge is fixed. Muiden, at the mouth, is splendid by the water, with an antique lock, recently restored at some expense. In the background is a castle and the first glimpse of the IJsselmeer, the inland sea.

A conical Jim Hawkins-type island, Pampuseiland, lies a mile or so offshore, and there is a marked channel out to it, with red topmarks on the western side and black to the east. I shall have more to say on IJsselmeerworthiness later; it can be choppy out here, and conditions are more akin to coastal sailing. Nor should a local hazard be overlooked, shown on the *waterkaart* as *Pier onder water* but, strangely, less succinctly described on the chart of the IJsselmeer itself.

Muiden is one of the refuges of the *botter* fleet, elderly sailing craft now used as yachts. They are constructed of wood, with low sterns and considerable beam. Their masts and fluttering pennants provide a reminder of the days when the IJsselmeer was the tidal Zuyder Zee, and the fishing fleet was hundreds strong. Jan de Hartog's *The Lost Sea* recaptures those days with gusto and charm, and ever since reading it I have been unable to look down on one of these wide flat vessels without thinking of the author, as a little boy, shut in the bow locker, while the best Liar, the storyteller of the fleet, wove his magical tale of the Mermaid.

There is a shipyard at Muiden also, while across the cobbled street near the lock is a bar *par excellence*. Good Dutch bars are not just havens of alcohol. You may have coffee in them, soup, chicken, or chips with mayonnaise on them, a disconcerting Dutch custom; you may play billiards, read from the pile of papers, engage in all manner of discourse in excellent English with a wide range of characters. I was in a Dutch bar once in which an extrovert man was playing a wild form of billiards, sweeping the bystanders with his cue and stamping alarmingly hard with his feet, considering that he had discarded his shoes in the common Dutch fashion. He wore a conical hat, perhaps from the nineteenth century, a big knitted scarf and a tweed suit several sizes too big for him. 'See that man there?', a Dutch companion remarked. 'Manager of the local bank.'

The last time I was in the bar at Muiden it was full of adolescent schoolgirls holding an immensely earnest meeting around the main table. The other tables are covered in a heavy carpet material; there are lowish lights, lots of dark wood, cuttings and mementoes around the walls. It is a nice place.

A useful illustration of the need to look at *waterkaarten* closely is provided by an alternative route into Muiden, the narrow direct Trekvaart, running from the direction of Amsterdam. Straight as a needle for several miles, this minor canal suddenly becomes convulsed in its last few metres, with a hairpin bend before a lift bridge and a small lock. A schoolboy wound the liftbridge for *Arthur* while another held up the traffic, but the lockkeeper came galloping out of his house at our approach, despite the chamber being open at both ends, with an apparently clear passage right through. The source of his concern became apparent as we squeezed by with a wafer thickness to spare on each side; it was 4.4 metres wide, a very narrow lock indeed.

Rupelmonde House on the Vecht, near Utrecht.

On the farther side of Muiden a similar canal runs parallel to the shore of the IJsselmeer, as far as Naarden. The Naarden town moats still remain, a remarkable star shape in plan. An outpost of Amsterdam, it was over-run in 1572 with brutal murder and torture by the Spanish forces. The Grote Kerk of Naarden built in 1440 also survives; with impeccable acoustics, it is used for a performance of the St Mathew Passion each Good Friday.

Amsterdam

A tour of Amsterdam's waterways is not for every craft. There are low bridges, involving the removal of wheelhouse or awning. In *Arthur*'s case, this was like a unison tossing of the caber. There is also something of a campaign to keep the visitor out. Large craft will be turned away; others receive a permit for a short stay, and there is a general tendency to refer one to a marina on the distant shore of the huge North Sea Canal which rages outside the Central Station, or to another, on the south bank of the same water, at a point of maximum disturbance from wash.

In practice, it is possible to moor in one of the small canals, the old town moats that run in concentric loops. Choose a quiet one, and a few days in Amsterdam can be pleasant indeed.

If approaching from the south, down the handsome River Amstel, there is an antique watergate, at which a small charge is levied for a week's visit. Those coming from the north can pay at a lock to the west of the Central Station, while the less law-abiding will get in for nothing through the Oosterdok, where the square-rigged sailing ship *Pollux* is moored.

There are many houseboats and Amsterdam, alas, has a proportion of scruffy ones. The situation worries many citizens, as does an increase in thuggery in this traditionally liberal city, but floating homes were still allowed for a purely nominal sum when I last visited, and this covered the supply of water and collection of rubbish. Later, when I bought the Dutch barge *Secunda*, we lay alongside a beautiful sailing vessel by the bus station; and I once found a tranquil mooring for *Arthur* in the Singel, the oldest of the city moats. We tied by accident outside the home of a prominent figure in Rembrandt's 'Night Watch'. Hearing this referred to over a loudspeaker, the crew popped up to find itself being earnestly photographed by sixty Oriental visitors on tour in a waterbus.

These craft are numerous and swift. If travelling the canals as I did, after dark in a small dinghy, have a care at the several blind corners. I was treated to such an adventure by a local enthusiast, who kept a motor barge out on the Amstel, and his dinghy outside the flat he had rented in the centre. Barge dinghies are tough. As we cannoned into a wall and ricocheted off a waterbus, I was thankful it was made of steel. He explained also the function of the several gates, and the lock into the system, to the west of the Central Station. These are all closed at night, to enable the levels to be adjusted and to give the canals a good flush through, in order to clear them of pollution.

Our tour took in the red light district, which crowds around a Hogarthian drain, a mass of bawdy signs and painted ladies in windows. From there we shot through a forest of concrete pillars beneath another part of the railway, and out into the North Sea Canal. There we were pursued by a police boat for travelling up the wrong side, but we evaded it and worked back through the lock. I learned afterwards that this also is forbidden.

Parts of the Amsterdam waterways are not what they were. An area has been insensitively filled in by the station and the adjoining houses demolished to make way for a new rapid-transit rail system from the polders formed by draining off the IJsselmeer. There have been strong protests, and the scheme is now curtailed, but much damage has been

done. Many of the traditional Amsterdam sights survive further south: Dam Square, the Muntplein and flower market. I like the Van Gogh Museum, the trams, a good bookshop out towards the Rijksmuseum, and the Tzucinski Cinema with its hand-painted wallpaper and splendid elaboration, not far from the Munt Tower at the inner end of the Singel.

Arthur *moored in the Singel in Amsterdam, once one of the city moats, built in concentric rings as the centre expanded.*

The approaches to Amsterdam (left). These watergates stand across the River Amstel; craft approaching from the south are vetted, and issued with tickets if a temporary stay is requested.

The Noordhollands and Nordsee Canals

The Noordhollands Canal is the old shipping route into Amsterdam, built when the Zuyder Zee silted. A direct link with the North Sea was impractical at the time; there was a lake in between and problems with the levels, so this longer canal was dug, to be opened in 1824, a fifty mile winding ribbon from bleak Den Helder. Nowadays, its traffic largely gone and several of the bridges fixed, it is a wistful, lonesome route across flat countryside. Old cannons act as bollards at its edges, a reminder of the days when sailing ships were warped around its corners. The odd sand barge ploughs along it still, so yachts should moor near bridges or the occasional cable ferry, where the traffic slows down.

Alkmaar, halfway along the course of the Noordhollands Canal, is an attractive town of spires and tiny stone bridges, with many sixteenth century mementoes. Once its citizens withstood a siege by Spanish troops twenty times their number. It is said that the siege was lifted under the threat of flooding the land and engulfing the surrounding army, and that the withdrawal prevented the drowning of the land. Today Alkmaar retains its cheese market, conducted with fancy ceremonial each Friday morning throughout the summer.

Further north the aspect becomes bleaker, with lonesome dykes along which the occasional cyclist doggedly creaks into the omnipresent headwind. There are cross-cuts for those bent upon Medemblik, running in woodland in part, deserted almost always. In these long straight drains there is a widespread feeling of straying into an eerie dream in which voyages last for ever.

Opened in 1876, and enthusiastically enlarged several times, the Noordsee Canal is now the direct thoroughfare running from Amsterdam to IJmuiden. It is wide, busy, and has three bends, none of them noticable. Since huge ships push along it, this is no place to linger. The western entrance is at IJmuiden with a complex of locks and docks said to be the biggest in the world. If not, they are awe-inspiring enough. The two on the southern side, Zuidersluis and Kleine Sluis, are customarily used by yachts. Once inside, a marina may be reached by crossing over to a point near the steelworks.

At eighteen miles overall the passage to Amsterdam is not a long one, but it is best accomplished in one shot, for several of the connecting routes are also busy, particularly that between Spaarndam and Haarlem. There are, however, moorings at Spaarndam itself, where one of the earliest locks in Europe was constructed, in the sixteenth century.

Despite the width of the Nordsee Canal, traffic upon it is expected to follow standard marine practice and 'keep to the right'. Pleasure craft must also keep to the side, and well clear of the shipping. The point is emphasized by grey police boats that harry the wayward.

In Amsterdam there are also towering ferries, which have a knack of hurling themselves forward at inconvenient moments. It is sometimes a toss-up between staying out in the stream and attracting the wrath of the Water Police, or of cutting close under a ferry likely to zoom forward without warning. Just beyond where they ply is the entrance to the Oosterdok, under a railway bridge, and here the travel-

Alkmaar

weary may tie to the nearest dormant barge and take stock. Another grey police boat, specially trimmed down for city use, may come along to chivvy as well, but statistically the odds are against it for an hour or so, and I have lain in here for three days without being bothered.

At the eastern end of the Nordsee Canal, just out of Amsterdam, are the Oranjesluizen, a trio of parallel locks out into the IJsselmeer. Busy in the week, less so at weekends,

they are run with po-faced efficiency, and the waiting traveller will be instructed by loudspeaker. Such directions, naturally enough in Dutch, can be difficult to follow, with doubts as to identity. Useful accessories are an enormous ensign, to emphasize Britishness, or the name of the vessel in large lettering. The word *jacht* will almost certainly be used, however, if you are in one. Alternatively, those unnerved by all these instructions can wait until a Sunday morning, when commercial traffic is light and co-operative Dutch yachtsmen will appear on the scene to explain.

THE NOORDHOLLANDS AND NOORDSEE CANALS

The Noordhollands Canal, once a major shipping route, now carrying little except the occasional sand barge. (Eric Coltham)

In the city centre

Panamanian steamer and small barge on the Nordsee Canal, now the major commercial route to Amsterdam, (Alex McMullen)

The IJsselmeer – Introduction

The IJsselmeer was formed in 1932 by damming the old Zuyder Zee. At the southern end of the great dyke, which is $18\frac{1}{2}$ miles long, stands a statue of Dr Cornelis Lely, the central figure and inspiration of the project. Huddled in his greatcoat and gazing inland, he makes an overwhelmingly romantic image. As a comparatively young man, secretary of a pressure group for the construction, Lely developed the scheme privately, caught the ear of the Prime Minister, and ultimately became a minister himself. In and out of office three times, he was sixty-three when his plans were approved, and had been dead three years before the last gap in the wall was plugged.

The sea broke in to form the Zuyder Zee in 1282, and so stayed exactly 850 years. During this time a tradition of seafaring developed, still evidenced by the buildings and local craft. Seamanship remains a requirement, for these waters are given to short steep waves, and there is a twenty-five mile fetch in which they can develop. Safe channels are provided within some of the polders of reclaimed land, and there are secure canals to several of the IJsselmeer ports; but the Lake itself provides good sailing for the reasonably prudent.

One area, the 50,000 acre Wieringermeer Polder at the western end of the dam, was reclaimed early. The German Army flooded it in retreat, but the land was pumped dry again in four months. The Northeast Polder was drained during the war, to reveal numerous wrecks and the remnants of mammoths, while Flevoland, the big new island in the south, was created in the 1950s. Another polder, the

The IJsselmeer at Staveren

Markerward, nears completion now, to take in much of the area between Enkhuizen and Flevoland, and although canals are left, both around and through, half the lake's area is now obliterated.

So great have been the changes wrought that there is now a society to stop it. Attention has been drawn to the strongly-rooted traditions and customs of the Zuyder Zee townships as sea-going and fishing communities, and to the sterility of life on the new polders. As in so many technical developments, man is confronted with the awkward choice of where to hold them in check.

There is still sufficient water left to provide some boisterous sailing, and although it is now fresh, rather than salt, and the eel and herring fisheries have come to an end, the atmosphere of the lake, with the waves slamming and the land a distant smudge upon the horizon, can still jerk at the vitals as sea sailing always has done. The average depth of the IJsselmeer is about 4 metres, and in many parts it is less. In fresh or strong winds it is particularly dangerous, for a wind blowing across such distances of shallow water produces a hostile sea. Craft should not venture upon it in doubtful weather; local enquiry is fervently recommended, and shipping forecasts should be listened to. Scheveningen Radio obligingly transmits them in English, and wavelengths and times are published in the frontispiece of Hydrografisch Chart 1810. In the case of the IJsselmeer, where new walls spring up rapidly and the bed of the lake is reconstructed before one's very eyes, it is most unwise to sail without the current edition.

The IJsselmeer – Western Shore

*Zuyder Zee fishing craft, preserved
and on display in The Pepper House
at Enkhuizen, built in 1625 and now
housing many paintings, models,
furnishings and reconstructed
interiors to commemorate life around
the shores of the lake when it was still
directly connected with the sea.
Symbols on the bows of the nearest
craft indicate registry at Marken and
Wieringen, both former islands, now
linked with the mainland by
polderization.*

The Afsluitdijk is the fundamental dam, resisting the sea at
the northernmost entrance to the gulf. A wide, solid rampart
with sloping sides, it bears a hypnotic motor road. For those
in a car it seems to go from nowhere to nowhere else, and
occasional viewpoints are provided, affording views of the
grey North Sea on one side and the grey IJsselmeer at the
other. The entry locks from the sea are at either end,
practical rather than cheerful places with concrete in
abundance and sheltering groynes for those waiting for the
sluices to open. It is difficult to realize now that the land at
the western end was once an island, Wieringen, connected
and drained before the Afsluitdijk was ever built.

Medemblik is the next harbour on the western shore,
altogether sprightlier, and bristling with yachts in summer
as all these ports now are. It is guarded on the seaward side
by Radboud Castle, one of several Hansel and Gretel
establishments around the coastline; this one, built in the
thirteenth century by the conquering Count Floris V, had
virtually collapsed in the nineteenth century but is now
neat and pristine, with gardeners to trim the verges of the
moat. For a day in September the streets of Medemblik are
given over to trotting matches, each horse pulling a single
rider on a lightweight racing sulky.

There is trotting also at Enkhuizen, which lies around the
next headland. At the harbour entrance is a double tower,
the Drommedaris of 1540, and the whole town is an antique.
When I first visited Enkhuizen Father Christmas had just
arrived too, by schooner, with a party of Moors (and I saw

him again in Medemblik, where he had acquired horn-rimmed spectacles and was riding on a donkey). The schooner was an old barge, converted back to sail after a lifetime of trade; this is a fad around the IJsselmeer where several such craft, with various rigs, sail on charter through much of the year.

Enkhuizen once had a population of 40,000, dwindling to 5,000 in the middle of the last century and now standing at around 15,000. This is a pattern around the old Zuyder Zee, which once had rich, powerful ports, busy trading centres with the Indies. Then they shrank to become fishing centres, before developing again as yachting harbours. But in the fishing days Enkhuizen alone supported 400 *botters*, and the life is excellently recalled at the large Zuyder Zee Museum, which is located in The Pepper House, a warehouse dating from 1625. Restored vessels, models, paintings and mocked-up interiors are all on display.

To supplement the old harbours, which are nowadays packed during the yachting season, there is a marina cut onto the foreshore, directly under the gaze of The Pepper House. A long training wall now faces Enkhuizen, a part of the latest polder, and for some time there has been a lock to let craft pass the new enclosure. Looking northeast, the distant shoreline of Staveren may be discerned on a clear day, a smudge of land with the odd blob upon it, a pumping station and some houses. A ferry runs across in summer.

While Enkhuizen still lies on the fringe of open water, the port of Hoorn, perhaps the grandest of them all, faces polderland across the entire horizon. Abel Tasman was born here; so was Coen, founder of what has become known as Djakarta. Cape Horn was named after Hoorn, by Schouten, who was born here and rounded the tip of South America in 1616; and it was at Hoorn itself that the Spanish flagship *Inquisition* was forced ashore and the fleet routed. Friezes on Hoorn's fine buildings record this victory.

In the days of the herring fleets any of several harbours

might be chosen by the crews of the Protestant *botters*, who would sail downwind to be sure of arriving for the Sunday services. Thus the harbour might be empty one weekend, packed solid the next. A vivid description of Hoorn under these conditions may be found, once again, in Jan de Hartog's *The Lost Sea*.

Edam, entered between twin moles and through an old

Lighthouse on Marken

Hoorn, once one of the great trading centres, now has its harbour largely occupied by yachts. Gabled, heavily decorated buildings recall former glories. (Theo Kampa)

lock, has a lovely narrow canal running through its centre. One has to play Hunt the Bridgekeeper here, since he operates several and may be at the far end of his beat. Local children will lead the enquirer to his door in the middle of the town, which also has a lavish town hall, and a museum in an old sea captain's house, as well as sixteenth century stained glass. Inevitably there is a cheese museum also. Just outside the town lies the connection with a small ditch, the Purmer Ringvaart, along which yachts may pass to Purmerend, a town of houseboats and council estates, where the Noord Holland Canal is joined.

Volendam, the next port down the coast, much promoted by the tourist board and heavily visited, is one of several townships in which local costumes are sported: baggy trousers and round black caps for men, black dresses with lace bonnets and other accoutrements for the ladies. This was a Catholic port, from which the *botters* used to fish while running before the wind, with a trawl net in tow. If they encountered the Protestants, who fished in pairs with a net in between, a dreadful tangle would ensue, with hard words and fighting to follow. Nowadays it is a yachting harbour, well buoyed as they all are, with occasional space inside for the determined summer visitor.

Offshore stands the former island of Marken, now connected by causeways. The water that they enclose bristles with nautical life in summer, a jamboree of tiny sails, airbeds and pedalos. Marken also has its traditional costumes, and a fine lighthouse, a reminder of Zuyder Zee days.

Should these local harbours be too busy, there is always trippery Monnickendam close by. Yachts throng in here too, but those prepared to push their way through will find a quiet mooring beyond the town, where a lock connects with a pleasant dyke running from Amsterdam.

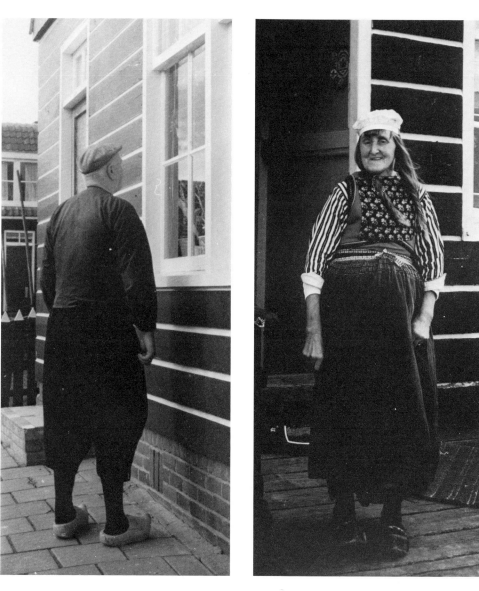

Volendam, bustling with visitors in the summer. (Theo Kampa)

Traditional costume at Volendam, once the Catholic fishing stronghold. (T. Thompson)

Around Flevoland

The old lock on the Vecht at Muiden, recently restored. Arthur *and a group of yachts work their way through, towards the IJsselmeer.*

Lock on the polder channel, south of Flevoland. (facing page)

As part of the reclamation scheme, navigable channels are left around each polder as it is created. Thus the one named Flevoland nestles as a large island, half a mile or so from the old lake shore; and it is possible to sail between them.

Arthur did this, setting out from Muiden on what was fortunately a calm day. A large expanse of water remains here, sufficient to frighten the Leeds & Liverpudlian pants off a short boat operator if the wind gets up. Later I was to cross the area again in a large better-equipped barge, on a wild, gusty day when the whitecaps were appearing and Pampuseiland seemed sheeted in spray.

Once inside the polder channel, however, there is greater protection. There are buoys to mark the way, and three large electrically operated locks at constrictions in the passage. As so often in Holland, no change in level is discernible at any of them, but the gates are dutifully closed at each end, and they take an unconscionable time to operate. There is little barge traffic, but a number of yachts in season, and the sight of one of these, distant upon the horizon, will be sufficient to make the keepers wait. And then another may appear.

It took *Arthur* two bumbling days to accomplish the passage, though it could, with greater application, be easily covered in one. There are various faded ports, old Zuyder Zee places such as Spakenburg and Elburg, while a wrinkly winding river, the Eem, allows barges to ascend the ten miles or so to Amersfoort, a bustling town with walls and moats. Spakenburg, an old fishing village where local costumes are still worn, retains its traditional shipyard, which repairs *botters* for enthusiasts. A man about nine feet high, dressed entirely in black and bearing a gaunt expression, turned up behind one of my crew in the local shop. The materialization practically sent him gibbering, and he had only called in for cigarettes.

Harderwijk has a dolphinarium and aspirations as a resort, although factories tend to dominate. Smoked eels are still on sale from its stalls, despite the demise of the industry; today's supply is brought in by air freight from Lough Neagh in Northern Ireland.

Elburg follows for the eastbound traveller, with a small frayed-at-the-edges harbour which belies its neat moat and walls. Both Elburg and Harderwijk retain their Fishgates, a combination of town gateway and lighthouse.

The wooden fishing botter *derived from an earlier type, the* schokker, *with a heavy, raked stem. Few* schokkers *survive, but a number of* botters *remain, preserved for private sailing. Here two* botters *reach up the channel inside one of the polders. The low flat foredeck severely restricts living accommodation.*
(Rob van Mesdag)

62

At the end of the sheltered channel there is another exposed area, the Ketelmeer, into which also flows the River IJssel. Long stone walls protect the entrance to this river, marked and lit at their outer ends. A substantial barge traffic works in and out.

On the northern side of the Ketelmeer is the entrance to another route, that leading by way of the Zwarte Meer to Northwest Overijssel. There is another long training wall here, which has to be rounded. If buying Waterkaart C, which covers the region, yachtsmen should check whether this wall coincides exactly with a fold in the map. It did on my copy, and I almost missed the way completely.

The Zwarte Meer is extremely shallow outside the buoyed channel, as a litter of stranded vessels will confirm on a busy sailing weekend. For those equipped with echosounder, lead line, or that much more reliable substitute a long bamboo pole, these shallows are tempting to lie in at anchor on a mellow summer night, but it is better to do so towards the western end, away from the constant din of dredging equipment and the wash of huge sand barges.

The Fishgate in Harderwijk. (Theo Kampa)

The Polder Canals

The canals inside Flevoland are strange waterways, long straight ditches entered from off the Ketelmeer. There, a lock will lower the voyager as he comes from outside, a most uneasy experience that is contrary to basic instincts; the average Briton is accustomed to ascending once he reaches land. There are views of pylons and crop sprayers on the rich new soil, while the occasional barge thumps about in search of agricultural cargoes. Farms are to be seen from time to time, and by tying to a concrete stage and tramping into a glass and concrete hamlet it is possible to whistle up a taxi for a journey to the Flevohof at Biddinghuizen. This is a big exhibition centre of modern farming methods: agricultural machines, concentration camps for hens, and so forth. In the similar press of people I got myself trapped in the tomato section on the hottest day of the year, and wondered if I could make it to the final glass door.

There is a different canal outlet to Lelystad on the northwest shore. This is the main town of Flevoland, widely acknowledged as a social disaster. It is an antiseptic place of flats and housing estates, laid out on a grid pattern. Time will perhaps lend it some mess and confusion and, paradoxically, a little more interest. It was this difficulty in creating a lively new atmosphere in the polders that led to the idea of a rapid rail connection and many nice old houses in Amsterdam have been demolished because of it. Doctor Lely would no doubt be perturbed by the memorial.

There is a vast work harbour outside Lelystad, a corral of walls made from blocks of broken stone. This is being incorporated in another inland channel as the next polder is added. In the meantime traffic from Amsterdam cruises outside, passing on to the wide open spaces of the remaining IJsselmeer. From here, wishing I had brought some seasickness pills, I once crossed in a yacht to Urk.

Early morning near Harderwijk. Herons and gulls line the rail.

Urk and the Noordoostpolder

Urk harbour

A motor yacht waits as a barge clears the lock at Marknesse on the route inland from Emmeloord.

Urk is much that Lelystad is not. It is a gutsy fishing village of a very old school, tough and intensely religious, a place where it is said you were pelted with stones if you arrived in a yacht on Sunday. Once it was an island; now it is linked to fresh land through pumping, but Urk fishermen still go far out to sea. There is a memorial to those who have been lost, with a statue of a woman in blowing skirts looking seaward. Around her, on stones, are the names of drowned men, and some of them are recent.

The harbour is a bustling one, full of fishing craft. Yachts are more welcome now, but must take their chance among the commercial stuff. Urk has several shipyards, including a picturesque one at the extreme end of the inner harbour. From here it is but a short step into the town, with painted wooden buildings and more traditional costumes. On Sundays still, this proudly Protestant town is closed up, and even on a weekday there is an odd but by no means unpleasant atmosphere about it. Only later did I discover

DIT MONUMENT WERD OPGERICHT
VOOR DE NAGEDACHTENIS VAN DE
IN DE GOLVEN OMGEKOMEN VISSERS
VAN URK
EN DE ELFDE MEI A. D. 1968 DOOR
H.M. KONINGIN JULIANA ONTHULD
— EN DE ZEE WAS NIET MEER —
OPENBARING 21 VERS 1 TOT 7

Memorial at Urk, and fishermen working in the harbour.

what accounted for it: the absence of cars, these being banned from the centre.

The canal inland from Urk is far more attractive than those of Flevoland. It lacks the same high banks, while age has mellowed it, providing rough edges, reeds and bulrushes. Again, the locks into this system are deep, descending ones, while there is some barge traffic to Emmeloord in the middle. A junction here gives access to a straight deep cut running directly northward to Lemmer, on the fringe of Friesland. This is the Lemstervaart, a claustrophobic dyke of brown muddy water running beside a main road.

To continue eastwards is a far more attractive course. There is a most picturesque lock at Marknesse, a small one by Dutch standards at 39 metres overall, with the inevitable lift bridge. Beyond this are pleasant pine woods, and a slight aura of tourist-consciousness, with dinky little mooring stages for yachts. There are barbecue stations, bench seats for picnickers and notice boards. Random mooring among the reeds is not encouraged here, because it disturbs the numerous marsh birds.

The final cuts in the polder channel are attractive indeed, with more woods, reeds and many water fowl, including such comparative rarities as the smew, one of the merganser family with a chestnut, thatched-looking head on the female. At dusk such birds abound, and this and the canals that follow are a naturalist's delight. A lock at the end leads to further wildlife sanctuaries, a series of winding attractive waterways along what used to be another edge of the IJsselmeer, through Vollenhove, Blokzijl and Ossenzijl.

Noordwest Overijssel

In this province the old fringes of the Zuyder Zee are now firmly embedded in the countryside. Had I not read otherwise, I would scarcely have guessed that Vollenhove and Blokzijl were once coastal towns. Vollenhove has a tight little haven, straight out of Toytown, tucked away behind a lift bridge in wilder less disciplined territory than that of the polders. It is easy to overlook and I only saw it myself while waiting for the bigger lift bridge across the main waterway outside. If delayed here and wind-blown, as *Arthur* was, it requires concentration to stay in the channel, which is noticeably shallow at the sides.

Blokzijl is a bigger fortified harbour, entered through lock gates in a gap in the outer wall and now permanently open. Inside, stately rows of houses face the water, a big expanse now partly filled with mooring pontoons. A charge is made for staying here, save out of season when there is no-one around to sell the tickets.

I have sculled a barge dinghy in this harbour (a remarkably easy task, since the Dutch provide a long bent oar which more easily remains in the socket). Progressing silently, I was able to come within feet of a heron digesting a large fish. Just over the walls hundreds of birds cluttered and wheeled around, and the canal outside the gates was covered in duck and geese.

At the far corner of the basin is a lock, another unexpected descent, worked by friendly keepers toiling over manual sluices. If in a barge, or other large vessel, a charge may be made for penetrating the next few miles of waterway, but it is a modest one, accompanied by the distribution of 'Welcome' leaflets and a presentation refuse bag. One senses, correctly, that further carefully ordered mooring places are to follow, with tables and trestle benches hewn from treetrunks, and discreet canisters for rubbish.

Looking north: the approaches to Friesland.

This winding canal route diverges several times, with links to the town of Steenwijk and more lakes, but the main line north passes through an agreeable holiday cottage area. The canal winds past men gathering reeds for thatching, and the odd volley on the horn is needed to get a slender swing bridge opened. Alongside, wind-pumps creak and there are mysterious little ditches into the marshes. The main forms of transport in this region are by boat or bicycle along the towpath, there being no convenient road.

Since there are numerous low lawns, and gaggles of moored dinghies, there is a speed limit throughout of 6 kilometres an hour, an unambitious walking pace designed to cut down wash. I saw it broken once or twice by hastening motor cruisers, which attracted black looks and shouts from the shore.

The village of Ossenzijl marks the border of Friesland, a good point at which to buy a Frisian courtesy flag. This is of red hearts, symbolizing lily leaves, on white stripes across a blue background. The gesture will be appreciated, Friesland having a similar standing to, say, Wales, with its own language, still spoken, and occasional demonstrations of independence. Frisian words appear alongside the Dutch on road signs, and English is not so widely spoken from here onward. There is no lack of hospitality; sometimes, in fact, the British visitor is singled out, and *Arthur*'s Red Ensign several times attracted a word of welcome. Comparatively few British visitors come so far on the waterways, which is a pity; Germans, on the other hand, visit Overijssel and Friesland in droves, so that the German ensign on small boats becomes almost as common as the Dutch.

Gathering reeds for thatch at Ossenzijl, Noordwest Overijssel. Transport in this region is by boat or by bicycle along the slender path beside the waterway.

Friesland

There is a spider's web of waterways across Friesland; hundreds if not thousands of miles of navigable canal linking many lakes, running through pretty villages and encircling the olde worlde towns. In summer the main watercourses throb with pleasure traffic; there are many visitors by boat, while practically all the locals can sail as if to the manner born. A friend told me how his sloop was drifting out of control beside a Frisian quay. There was only one soul about, a dumpy middle-aged lady tramping by with a shopping bag. He threw her a rope and, without batting an eyelid, she took a turn around a bollard, surged the line and brought them to a halt.

The Prinses Margriet Canal is the main highway, running from the IJsselmeer near Lemmer, where craft enter through a very large lock. Thus northbound barges tend to be encountered in convoys, as each lockful is released. As there are speed limits in several sections the barges do not travel quickly, merely irresistibly, up a buoyed channel where it passes through the lakes. If joining from a side canal it is easy enough to see oncoming traffic, for the countryside is flat indeed, with random clumps of trees and the occasional large farmhouse with a big roof, reminiscent of a partially-completed pyramid. The theory of these roofs is that all the farm departments are grouped under one shelter, for greater efficiency and heat saving; though in practice other buildings tend to be tacked alongside.

There is a further lock along the way, near Terhorne, but this is only used occasionally, for flood control. Traffic signals indicate one's course of action, which is generally a slow trundle forward. The Sneekermeer, on which Terhorne lies, is a favourite place for dinghy racing, the commercial barges bashing on between rows of coloured sails which stand out like shark's teeth on a sunny day. Farther north again is Grouw, a big marina centre, then Suawoude, where the van Harinxma Canal is joined. This is the other big barge route in Friesland, a wide, deep, fairly straight waterway with high bridges and steady traffic. It runs from Harlingen on the coast past Franeker and Leeuwarden, the chief town of the province. Harlingen is a busy port, with fishing craft as well as barges. Franeker is noted for its buildings, including a sixteenth century town hall and an eighteenth century planetarium built by a local woolcomber. Leeuwarden is a centre for cattle buying, and also has its quota of aged buildings. It has never greatly inspired me, perhaps because I once got stuck there, years ago, in a hire-boat. After venturing into the centre through many lift bridges, I discovered that they did not open again the following day, a Sunday. This is a common practice in Friesland.

Sneek, pronounced Snake, is right at the centre of the system, another town that may be penetrated by boat. It is possible to moor near the middle, with the turreted brick watergate in prospect. Occasionally a barge will glide in too, to unload grain, although the main wharves are just outside the town on the direct route to the Sneekermeer.

There is a regatta week every summer, and an annual competition between *skutsjes*. These are trim sailing craft,

somewhat like a *tjalk* in outline but lighter and finer, and each of the more important Frisian towns will enter one. The races do not all take place on the Sneekermeer; the venue is moved around throughout the week to incorporate open water sailing as well as some vigorous no-holds-barred stuff in narrow channels. The sight of one of these fiercely handled vessels luffing another into a mark boat or thundering full tilt up the bank can make the sailing purist's blood run cold. So may the spectacle of the crew, in blatant defiance of the rules, hurling their stone ballast overboard to lighten ship when running before the wind. *Skutsje* racing generally takes place in the first two weeks of July and is worth enquiring after, particularly if visiting by boat, which will afford a grandstand view.

Makkum and Workum both lie on the IJsselmeer shore, with entry buoys for guidance. Each is charming – Makkum is a pottery centre – and from either one it is but a short journey to attractive Bolsward, up thin twisting dykes.

Hindeloopen, further south, has moorings in the outer harbour, but the town canals are only for the very tiny. The IJsselmeer needs lifeboats too, and that at Hindeloopen for many years bore the name *Arthur*. Hindeloopen is also a centre for rose-painting and decorated woodwork somewhat akin to the British canal tradition, although often superficial by the standards of earlier years. If Leeuwarden should be visited for nothing else, it is worth enquiring if the Frisian Museum of that town still has on display a carved rocking-cradle from Hindeloopen. This, dating from the eighteenth century, bears paintings from the Old Testament, and wonderful decoration.

Staveren is the next town down the IJsselmeer shore, a faded place with a large harbour. The Legend of Staveren is of a local woman, a power figure in the area, who ordered her best captain to bring the finest cargo he could find. Being of a practical Dutch nature he brought wheat, but the lady's response was one of fury, and she had the entire load dumped in the Zuyder Zee. There it formed a shoal which blocked the harbour mouth and ruined both herself and Staveren's future.

There is a statue of her, in pointed hat, upon the harbour wall. It is a very small statue, as if Staveren did not wish to be associated too strongly with the memory. The shoal to the south of the town is still known as the *Vrouwezand*, the Woman's Sand, and one might deduce that the mighty mansions of greater days would be found near this point; but no trace of them remains.

More recently, Staveren was the launching point for V2 guided missiles under German occupation. In truth, the place does have something of a gloomy air, although I came to know it well and found several endearing points.

The outer harbour and the canal system beyond now have separate entrances, for the lock that once gave access to the old town canal has now been filled in. An attractive pottery

Viewed from a lesser waterway, a large barge makes her way down the Prinses Margriet Canal. (left)

Stront *race on the Friesland meers near Workum. (Theo Kampa)*

plaque remains just visible above the tipped earth, and the town canal is now an attractive dead end, culminating in a vigorous little barge yard where craft of all types and sizes are hoisted briskly in and out of the water by means of sideways slips. Nobody minds having a barge moored outside their front door down here, and in the very street sailing enthusiasts are to be found planing masts or shaping leeboards.

There are little townships dotted inland, like islands, as they once must have been when more of the land was swamp. Although the odd motor car tootles about, and there is a general prosperity and an orientation towards tele-vision, there is also a strong connection with the Middle Ages in the region, particularly under dark flat skies, out of

Sailing on a botter. (Theo Kampa)

Sneek

Mixed traffic on the Prinses Margriet Canal outside Lemmer. Concrete screens protect unladen barges from the wind while manoeuvring for the lock, just out of picture at the left.

Stadhuis or town hall, Sneek

season. Somewhere in each of the settlements, in Warns or Balk or Lemmer, there is a corner, a group of buildings, or perhaps a barn painted in dull rusty red, that throws back directly to mysterious times before accurate recording, a feeling I now find rare in Britain. In this part of Friesland, and certainly in winter months, it is a sensation so strong that it almost vibrates.

Heerenveen, not a scintillating place, lies on the eastern

extreme of the Frisian network. It has glass tower blocks, and despite often providing the winning *skutsje* crew, its canals are largely closed. *Arthur* was briefly shut in here, between the railway bridge and the town's remaining hairpin bend, around which a barge had suddenly appeared. After turning the corner, which she did by going ahead and astern many times, she bore down upon us, bow high in the air, the wheelhouse invisible. But miraculously she wriggled past, her skipper leaving the wheel meanwhile in order to polish away a speck of dirt he must have seen on the sidedeck. The moral of this meeting is the old one of the inland waterways: there is always someone bigger than

Unloading grain at Leeuwarden.

yourself, and you will meet him unexpectedly, on a blind corner.

The railway bridge here is operated by the signalman, who has to find a gap between the frequent trains. Since the locomotives pick up power from overhead wiring these structures are complex. If arriving at a bad time, the signalman will generally lean from his eyrie to indicate when he can next open the bridge, but few craft have to wait for more than half an hour.

When I last passed through Heerenveen, another canal was being dug outside the town, a bypass waterway designed to eliminate both the bend and the bridge. The old section will then presumably fall into relative disuse, and the town's canals will support nothing larger than dinghies, or punts bearing potted plants.

Typical Frisian farmhouse, at Woudsend near Staveren.

Main line railway bridge, Heerenveen.

An empty barge encountered at Heerenveen.

An Escape from the Crowd:
the Tjonger Canal and its Connections

Finding Friesland rather crowded one summer, I was fortunate to be aboard a motor yacht exploring its outer fringes. Admirable though the *waterkaarten* are, they do not cover the whole of the Netherlands. There are numerous little canals outside their scope, some shown on small-scale maps but now closed, others in doubt. Some detective work in E. E. Benest's three volume *Inland Waterways of the Netherlands* reveals numerous unsuspected, allegedly navigable canals, and maps at the back of each book show their whereabouts.

The survival of several of them was hinted at in the *Almanak voor Watertoerisme*, the worthy two volume set produced by the ANWB. Unfortunately it is in Dutch, which compels a degree of brain damage in extracting lock and bridge opening times. In the case of the Tjonger Canal branching off to the east, its information was of a basic kind; a sketch map and the bald details of lock sizes. This bore some promise.

The Tjonger edges away from the popular system at a point near Heerenveen. At first its banks are modestly occupied by moored motor cruisers, but their ranks soon diminish and lonesomeness sets in. The main railway line from Leeuwarden establishes a sort of frontier point, for the bridge here is fixed. The boat I was on bore a large radar scanner on the wheelhouse, and this had to be unscrewed

A barge carrying peat on one of the smaller canals, in the region of Sneek.

and transplanted elsewhere. Thereafter we voyaged in solitude.

The canal ascends through three locks to join the splendidly named Opsterlandsche Compagnonsvaart, an equally obscure and wild waterway running between Friesland and the province of Drenthe. All these locks we found in fair order, with a trim keeper's house alongside each, sporting red and white decorated shutters and neatly trimmed gardens. In a region of little traffic it is not surprising to find a keeper absent and the lock under the control of a maniacal dog. Having a morbid fear of rabies at the time, induced by posters at English Customs points, I had to stay rooted to the spot until one of the lock-keepers returned. It was a long wait, and the pride of both parties was somewhat dented by the end of it.

By Dutch standards there is a substantial ascent at each lock, of four or five feet at least, while the system of pushing the gates open with a pole makes an energetic departure from advanced technology. Further features of these locks are that the gates are staggered in relation to one another, not taking up the entire width of each chamber, while at least one of the keepers, I am afraid, was of the outlook that is slightly annoyed because there are no boats, and even more annoyed when one turns up. Certainly we met no other vessel although commercial traffic was alleged. Since bridge clearances were 3.50 metres and lock lengths 29 metres only, these must be small barges, if they still survive. While manoeuvring at the topmost junction, our twin-screwed gunboat ran higgledy-piggledy over a lot of tree roots and other buried muck; so anything over 1.30 metres in draught is also pushing her luck up here.

The Opsterlandsche Compagnonsvaart is similar in character, but shrinks to even more drainlike proportions. For some miles it runs beside straight country roads, with elegant larger houses for each keeper, the sort that stockbrokers might fancy in Surrey. In its later stages it becomes little more than a duck stream, meandering across a bright green meadow before straightening out for a final lock in the village of Gorredijk. The lock is in the centre of the town, and the keeper a font of good cheer who plied us with leaflets and gave us a flag to celebrate the passage. There is apparently a lobby to keep this route open. I wish it success.

A continuation leads to Oldeboorn, a little town with bell tower and jolly houses, then Akkrum, which is more of a builder's yard sort of place, and arid. There are tight angular wriggles under the swing bridges here, so that a barge could barely squeeze through; but they do, because we met one. A few yards on lies Terhorne and the popular Sneekermeer once again.

Groningen

The capital of its province, and a town of fine squares and mansions, Groningen is a point where numerous waterways meet. Canals are mixed up in its streets, with many vantage points for barge fetishists. If passing through by boat some enquiry may be necessary, as it is normal to close the bridges on Sundays, or during rush hour. Even when the routes are open it is wise not to hoot too stentoriously while waiting: one keeper often works several bridges, and the poor chap may still be closing the last.

The big Starkenborgh Canal, an extension of the Prinses Margriet Canal and the main route for large barges to Delfzijl and the River Ems, bypasses the town. If arriving up it from the west there is a branch into the city from Dorkwerd, where a shaded lock, remarkably French in atmosphere, gives access to a smaller canal. After passing some construction sites and a bit of light industry, this becomes lined with the splendid residences and warehouses of Groningen itself.

The town canals are not all great places to lie, since hefty vessels come sliding along them, bringing a temporary paralysis to the road traffic. The canals in the inner city form a square, those on the western and southern sides being the main through routes, the others often occupied by houseboats and sundry small craft. The best mooring is perhaps on the southern side of this square, where the canal widens in a cutting outside the railway station.

It is tempting to describe the countryside around Groningen as flatter than the rest; certainly it has a bleaker

Waiting for the bridge-keeper, Groningen centre.

and, to me, less attractive quality than Friesland. Wild, strange little canals, many of doubtful navigability, spread across the province to the north and down into the southeast. In an early painting showing women working in the fields of Drenthe, which is actually the next province, van Gogh has captured the peaty fields and weird light of the whole of northeast Holland. In my various pursuits of barges I have tramped about this area in winter, seriously wondering whether it is day or night. On a clouded afternoon the area of sky seems overwhelming; there is a perpetual dusk.

Those journeying east may take the big Eems Canal to Delfzijl and the mouth of the Ems. Coasters come up this canal, as far as the docks east of Groningen. It is straight and purposeful, not a route to linger on.

Warehouses, shops and mansions are pleasantly intermingled by the Groningen waterways.

Meals in Holland

Holland offers substantial meals rather than gastronomic nuances. Traditionally, fish is a good bet, and it can be well served. There are pricey restaurants in every town, but few that compel hushed voices under a blanket of Ruritanian ostentation. They usually give fair value, since the portions served are generous to the point of enforced gluttony. There are also numerous Indonesian restaurants, serving 'rice tables' and other specialities, which tend to dish up a mixture of the standard Indian and Chinese food found in England. With the exception of an excellent meal in Hellevoetsluis, and a good one in Amsterdam, I have found them rather boring, although once again the quantities are large.

At the lowest end of the scale are numerous snack-bars, selling meatballs or sausage, while many coffee-cum-beer bars will produce the same, plus soup. But for a basic, sturdy meal, served with reasonable style in pleasant surroundings, the Dutch railway restaurants take some beating. To the visitor accustomed to haggling with ladies in nylon overalls in his own country, and wielding plastic cutlery, it is a revelation to find a smart waiter with a napkin over his arm, capable of speaking several languages, prepared to bring hot food to a comfortable table. This is a commonplace on the State railway system, and the rooms themselves are often pleasant too. Groningen has a good one, with heavy timber panelling and an air of Graham Greene and trans-Continental travel before the war. The prices are reasonable, and the food good.

Joining the Boat – Rail Travel

Arthur's crews would change week by week. Friends from work, relatives, girlfriends, mums and children would come traipsing out on the overnight ferry to an arranged timetable. My normal practice is to map out a schedule, do a list of those joining on particular dates, and tell the people concerned to keep in touch with one another, so that if there is a change in plan, I then only need to telephone one of them. Telephoning is less of a burden in Holland than in France, and it is often possible to dial right through, on a practical system whereby your money rests in a glass container and dissappears in proportion to the time consumed.

Occasionally my friends would press to come by car. As indicated earlier, this is not a good idea; they will not finish in the place they start from, and the voyage tends to become a tedious motoring holiday. In the Netherlands in particular there is no necessity, for the rail system is first rate. Trains connect and they run to sensible timetables, at the same number of minutes past the hour, every hour, and to the same times on Sundays. The conductor who sells the tickets often acts as porter as well. The trains are comfortably full, but there is usually a seat; the conductor announces the name of each coming station on a loudspeaker, while the tickets themselves have a map of the system on them. When you change trains the connection often comes rolling in on the other side of the platform.

Nor are they expensive. The system is heavily subsidized. It is cheaper than driving, as rail travel should be; convenient and civilized. I sometimes had to work hard to persuade *Arthur*'s crews of this, but they usually concurred after trying. They could catch an evening boat train from London, have a night's sleep on the ferry, and be on board *Arthur* in mid-Friesland the following lunchtime. People undergo more travail to keep a yacht on the English south coast.

South of Assen the canal dwindles. A 26 metre sand barge just squeezes through one of the locks. (facing page)

From Groningen to Zwolle

Between Groningen and Assen the canal is broad, concrete lined, but with comparatively little traffic. The odd 600-tonner lies at a gravel wharf, the occasional *spits* comes haring down; there is just sufficient to make careful mooring necessary. There are also several locks, big deep ones under electric control and with bollards recessed into their sides. Some visitors use doubled lines, around each bollard and back to the boat; I prefer a single one with a noose on it, provided it is heavy enough to be swung onto and flipped off each bollard in turn. If a lock is violent, a second rope can be secured to the next bollard up, and the use of single lines here makes them less likely to tangle.

This passage, southward from Groningen, took us once again outside the scope of the *waterkaarten*. I therefore relied on Born's *Schipperskaart*, a useful overall map of the Dutch system showing all locks and grading waterways by size. The canal to Assen had obviously postdated it: Born's shows it as small and narrow, and the canal that follows as reasonably broad. The reverse is the case, the Drentse Hoofdvaart, as it becomes known, is another little canal, like the Tjonger and the Opsterlandse Compagnonsvaart. The latter comes across to join it south of Assen. Maybe it will all be widened, as the Groningen-Assen stretch recently was, to make a direct deep route to the south, but at present it is tiny, with hand-wound locks. From time to time even smaller overgrown waterways creep off to the east, enshrouded in reeds and thicket. In theory they cross the German border, but I learn that they are now closed.

For many miles the Drentse Hoofdvaart runs alongside a busy motor road, which can be a trial, and as this canal also

Dredging on the Zwartemeer. (right)

The Drentsche Hoofdvaart, midway between Assen and Meppel. Despite the sparseness of traffic, all locks are manned.

is not covered in a *waterkaart* it is useful to acquire the local Michelin maps to pick out a mooring for the night. One such is on a rare slight bend, where the roadway diverges briefly and the noise from it diminishes: a chance to be taken.

Small cargo barges are getting rarer now, after the determined government drive to clear away anything under 350 tons, but I came across three on this canal, small motorized *tjalks* carrying sand, creeping along in the manner of narrow boats, with defensive expressions on the faces of the families on board. They survived in trade here because the locks were small at 26.5 metres, with a depth in the channel of little over 1.50 metres. In theory there is a speed limit on these minor canals of 6 kilometres an hour, and I doubt if these loaded craft could manage more in such a tight channel.

Meppel, Zwartsluis, Hasselt and Zwolle are the next towns southwards, barge centres the lot of them. The tiny canal from Assen debouches into a much bigger scene at Meppel, where large craft from the south come in to unload wheat. The stream to Zwartsluis is known as the Meppeler Diep, an attractive river, and not far to one side of it is a complex of lakes and islands in Noordwest Overijssel. There are supposedly deep channels across these lakes, but I have run sensationally aground in one, in a vessel drawing half of the 2.3 metres indicated. The lesson I learned was always to cross on the upwind side, since the buoys get blown across a channel on their mooring cables, and it can be tedious indeed to extract yourself from soft silt when held into it by the wind. If obliged to give way under the 'rule of the road' and pass closer to the downwind mark, it becomes neccesary to shave quite close to the oncoming vessel. If her skipper is sensible he will be cutting close to the upwind markers too, but those in shallow draught boats are not always aware of the consequences. If possible it is better to wait at the beginning of such a channel, until it is clear of oncoming craft.

Zwartsluis has picturesque barge moorings, jammed in under lofty trees. There are lovely views on a clear morning, out across to the Zwarte Meer, speckled here and there with gleaming sails. This stream runs to Hasselt and Zwolle, and the lock into it at Zwartsluis is commonly open at each end. It should not be swept through with too great a display of elan, since the corner is a blind one and commercial craft are now big indeed.

Hasselt is the sort of place where you get welding done, or gearbox oil provided, having climbed over numerous old scows to reach it. Zwolle, which follows, is an ancient stronghold, with a navigable moat. It is quoted all over the Dutch waterways as a good place for buying second-hand barges, although when I went there were none at all. The main canal bypasses it now, through a big lock, before bursting out into the IJssel.

The IJssel – Buoyage and Beacons

A swift river, the IJssel is fun to descend but a slog for upcomers. A branch of the Rhine, it flows into the IJsselmeer past Kampen, where barges hurtle, without the faintest intention of slowing down, towards a lift-bridge containing a traffic jam. Somehow the cars always manage to disperse in time.

Kampen is a rich city, with turreted gateways; a popular place for commercial craft to lie. If moored there in something smaller, double all ropes and put the crew under hypnosis, as the fleet departs early in the morning, to be at Zwolle when the lock opens. This is usually at six o'clock in summer, so the action starts at about five. I have been woken here at this hour by the roar of an unsilenced winch motor ten feet away, accompanied by violent eddies as the anchor of a large barge was lowered and raised several times, in order to get the flukes stowed properly.

The IJssel is another blue flag waterway, but since it is comparatively shallow and has several tight bends there are no mighty pushers or larger Rhine barges; instead a succession of medium operators come whirling down. If required to pass on the 'wrong' side they will readily do so, flying their own blue flags in acknowledgment.

There are numerous groynes stretching out from the banks, their tips marked by *kribbakens*, posts with triangular topmarks. Those on the starboard hand of craft ascending have their points upward, those to port point down. There is normally little merit in the distinction, since the relationship is obvious – save at the mouth of the river

Kampen has several city gates and mansions beside its busy waterside.

itself, where other channels run nearby, and on the occasional upstream islet, where they show which side to pass. The *kribbakens* come into their own when the river is in flood and the groynes are covered. In times of drought, and for deep-laden vessels, *bolbakens* are of greater value. These are posts with a different topmark, red, white and blue, like giant Loyalist lollies. Get two in line, and you are in the deep water channel. Also useful, as on so many of the Great Rivers, are kilometerage posts, which like *bolbakens* may be checked against the *waterkaart*.

It is said that the current of the IJssel becomes stronger the higher up one goes, but in my own experience it is reasonably strong all the way. The IJssel never matches the German Rhine; it merely retards insistently, in average conditions running at around three knots. There was once a small canal alongside, the Apeldoornskanaal, which reduced the agony of the ascent. It is closed now, although its entrances may still be perceived.

There are good moorings alongside at historic Deventer and steeped-in-history Zutphen, both well worth exploration. Though traffic on the river does not continue after nightfall, most barges make fast on the darker side of dusk. It is well, if mooring at these main river quays, to display a riding light through this period, and not to occupy the obvious berths. Almost all vessels will lie facing upstream, although, if necessary, barge masters make an excellent job of the running moor. If tied up under their sterns, be prepared for a rude awakening in the early dawn, when the wash will hit you.

Both towns have Industriehavens, as well as marinas, while Zutphen is the entry point to an unenticing network of big, straight commercial canals. The countryside of the IJssel, for the most part grassy meadows, acquires a few hillocks towards the top end, where the next section of the waterway, known as the Pannerdens Canal, connects with the main body of the Rhine near the German border. Skippers accustomed to blue-flagging and hugging the

inside of the appropriate bends should not do so if they wish to turn towards the North Sea at IJsselkop, the point where the IJssel ends. This can be a bedlam of barge traffic, which left hand bank huggers will be obliged to cross. Far better to hold the outside of the final IJssel bend and slip neatly around the point into the Neder Rijn, which flows westward, past Arnhem.

THE IJSSEL – BUOYAGE AND BEACONS

The IJssel at Kampen

Groynes and beacons on the IJssel, a relatively shallow and fast running river, the northernmost tributary of the Rhine.

Bargeman and his wife adjusting hatch covers on a 350 ton péniche or spits. These, and smaller craft, ply into many of the branches and harbours adjoining the main system.

The Neder Rijn and Lek, and Pendulum Ferries

Of all the Great Rivers, this route is the gentlest, for it has been equipped with barriers and locks, which slow the current. There is a good quay at Arnhem, rebuilt now after the destruction of 1944. Here also is a typical barge chandler, a source of stout rope and gear oil in 40 gallon drums, as opposed to the little polythene bottles found in the yachty centres.

Despite this quay and the gentility of the river, the Neder Rijn can be difficult to moor in, with few side canals and a heavily groyned, rather bony shoreline. One finishes up at the stagings near each lock. If staying here, rather than merely waiting for the lock chamber to be prepared, it is the custom to lie well back, at the farthest end of a staging. The locks themselves are very big, while the radial gate structures of the nearby weirs are lofty and striking.

At the crossing with the Amsterdam–Rhine Canal, referred to earlier, the Neder Rijn changes its name and becomes the Lek, flowing on to join the Noord near Krimpen.

A feature of the river is the pendulum ferry, which operates on an age-old principle. The ferry herself is tethered to a cable, anchored to a point in mid-channel, well upstream. By angling the vessel, she can be steered from one side of the river to the other, swinging on the cable like a pendulum, and propelled by the action of the current. A disadvantage of this otherwise admirable system is that it is possible for the unknowledgeable or distracted to run into the cable. It is accordingly marked with floats, or small

boats, which run to and fro in the river in the same fashion. When the ferry is at the bank, half the river is barred; when

Inside the Merwede Canal at Vianen.

*Water level control gates on the Lek,
seen from an adjacent lock cut.*

*Under sail on the Haringvliet: a
modern steel yacht related to a
traditional working boat, the
grundel.*

it is on the move, the danger area will change. The issue can be complicated by vessels coming the other way, and a golden rule of inland voyaging applies: if in doubt, hold back.

One of the pleasantest moorings is at the entrance to the Merwede Canal at Vianen, entered through an old brick lock. At weekends in particular, this canal provides a quiet tree-lined route to Gorinchem on the bustling Merwede. It has windblown trees and a rural atmosphere, while, unusually for Holland, the swing-bridges are manually operated, and one can contrast the purpleness of complexions as the keepers toil at the controls.

The Southern Estuaries

Those coming across the sea to the Netherlands will be attuned to the notion of sandbanks and tidal currents, to the tendency of incoming swells to steepen and pile up as they hit shoal waters. The outer approaches to the southern estuaries are not to be taken lightly.

Another difficulty in the southwest of the country is that the Dutch keep altering it. Huge dams are constructed between promontories, rivers diverted, once-remote islands are now connected by causeways and bridges, new canals appear almost overnight. Some of these areas are salt, some fresh, but it is often difficult to tell which is which. Vistas of sand provide a clue, and there are buoys in all directions, but it is the currents that spring the main surprise. Sometimes the whole tidal pattern has been reversed; in other cases the water ebbs away through some secondary channel across a peninsula.

This is the Delta Plan in earnest, a programme of land protection, rather than land reclamation, but on a mighty scale. Undertaken without a direct profit motivation, it is nonetheless transforming the country.

The Haringvliet, the first 'estuary' south of Rotterdam and the Nieuw Waterweg or New Waterway, is a classic example of the changes that the Delta Plan has wrought. There is a big dam at the mouth, with a road across it, a museum at the mid-point extolling its considerable virtues, and a lock at the southern end, with well-protected

harbours at its entrances. From here, travelling inland, there is buoyage on the conventional pattern, until the Spui is entered. This is a natural waterway, running through from Dordrecht; such tidal stream as now remains enters the Haringvliet through it and accordingly the buoyage in the Spui is suddenly reversed. Dutch chart no. 1807 reduces the possibility of nervous breakdown.

Middelharnis, on the southern shore of the Haringvliet, still has avenues of poplars such as those painted by Hobbema. It can be reached by locking into a long narrow canal, while Hellevoetsluis, on the northern side, is an old Napoleonic harbour that contains a modern marina. Once it was the packet boat port for Harwich, and it offers a lovely mooring with a nautical flavour just inside the entrance moles, and before the first swing bridge into the town. As in most of these harbours, a man comes along with a ticket machine on summer evenings, but a mooring here is well worth the price. There are other moorings of marina quality in Hellevoetsluis, in a separate harbour to the west, and in the old Voornsche Canal, which is entered through a lock. This is now a cul-de-sac, as I once discovered while trying to enter from the Rotterdam end, which is now blocked off.

To reach the next estuaries southward it is necessary to pass through the big locks at Willemstad, at a point where the Haringvliet has merged into the Hollandsch Diep. Willemstad town is friendly, with moorings by the old fortress moat, but the locks are large and daunting. If in a yacht, it is wise to wait at the back of any pack of barges and, on the safety-in-numbers principle, to go where the Dutch yachts go. My own passage through these chambers was lightened by talking to a keeper who went to Congleton in Cheshire for his holidays. He knew the Macclesfield Canal better than I did. I thought of Bosley Locks, seven feet wide and set among hills, and reflected on the structures of Willemstad, huge, and in an area of absolute flatness.

The stretch of water south of Willemstad, known as the Volkerak, and then the Krammer, is more fiercely tidal than

the Haringvliet. Much of its traffic now disappears into a new canal, cut directly towards Antwerp, and boring, as such a straight-line track might suggest. The old barge route is the dramatic one, still worth following; into the narrows at Zijpe, through which the current continues to scorch, before bursting out again between the sandbanks of the Ooster Schelde, the Eastern Schelde.

If lying for the night at harbours such as Bruinisse, just north of the Zijpe, a big allowance must be made for tidal fall, despite the presence of a dam to seaward. This wall

One of the locks into the Oosterschelde gives an idea of the scale of engineering on the Southern Estuaries. (Theo Kampa)

Harbour entrance at Hellevoetsluis, once the departure point for the packet to Harwich, now on a non-tidal estuary. Many of the town's Napoleonic fortifications remain. (left)

merely isolates the area known as the Grevelingen, and together with another, several miles further west, it creates a non-tidal section at the estuary mouth. There is a lock into it at the eastern or 'inland' end, and it is good for sailing; but there is no lock to seaward, and the Grevelingen is a nautical cul-de-sac.

When I last passed through the Ooster Schelde it remained a dangerous place of sandbanks and tides, with a tendency for heavy swells to build in an onshore wind, but needless to say, the entire estuary will be dammed off eventually.

The Ooster Schelde is crossed by the Zeelandbrug, a concrete road viaduct five kilometres long and striking to behold, particularly when it glints in the sun above the gold of the exposed sandbanks. Its clearances are generous, though not sufficiently so for all sailing craft, which must wait for the opening of a movable span once every two hours, during daytime. Nearby, on the northern shore, is the lovely preserved town of Zierikzee, approached up a long canal. There are hospitable moorings for small craft at its end. A town of spires and gateways, Zierikzee is dominated by the Monster Tower of Saint Lievens, 200 feet high, still less than a third of the stature intended when work began in the 1450s.

Between the Eastern and Western Schelde estuaries is a long peninsula with several ports, and three canals running across it. The easternmost of these is the new direct link to Antwerp, with big locks, the Kreekraksluizen, approached down a well buoyed channel. The old main route was through locks at Wemeldinge, under direction from a loudspeaker, into the Zuid Beveland Canal. This is a Devil-take-the-hindmost dyke, about four miles long, with nowhere to stop save at either end. There used to be bedlam at these points, as barges came tramping in steady procession between the sands to muster at the quays. Some still do. The smaller commercial craft fly banners at the masthead, like knights in tournament, and this enables them to be seen above gates and walls – a useful tip for all boat owners with a sense of self-preservation, and a particularly useful one on yachts which might otherwise be obscured beneath the high bows of unladen craft.

A wrinkled lake within the northern shore of Beveland and Walcheren leads to Veere and thence by the Kanaal door Walcheren to Vlissingen. Veere, once tidal, is now the focal point of safe, sheltered sailing. It retains the attractive houses of its great days when in the fifteenth century it thrived on its Scottish connection through marriage between van Borselen, a Dutch tycoon, and James I's daughter. It then imported wool, and 20,000 people lived there. A recent population figure for Veere was 1,200 only.

On the canal southward lies Middelburg, somewhat knocked about in the last war. The abbey was destroyed in 1940, while bombing broke the dykes and let in the sea during 1944. But much has been restored, and is architecturally stimulating. There are good basins in which to lie.

Vlissingen or 'Flushing' on the northern shore of the Schelde is a common port of entry. As everywhere in the Netherlands, formalities are minimal; pleasure craft are widely understood, and liked. The harbour entrance is used by a highly organized ferry service, which brings cars across from Breskens, and the entrance lock is just to the west of the ferry terminal. As at all harbours, craft approaching should never aim to cut the harbour walls close; there is a risk of tidal set, which through miscalculation could smash a vessel against them, and the helmsmen of other craft may be unsighted. There can also be an ugly swell at this point; indeed the Schelde as a whole is not to be trifled with. Craft approaching from the interior can be at great risk in poor weather conditions. I have seen a 1,000-ton tanker barge in serious trouble at the mouth of Flushing harbour, rolling heavily with waves breaking over her, and being set by tide onto a broken stone wall. In this instance a harbour tug was able to dash out, put a line aboard and tow her in.

Having struck the appropriate notes of doom, I must add

that we took *Arthur* down the inner Schelde in conditions of pancake flatness, although I had taken the precaution of listening to the BBC shipping forecast first of all. The winds,

Zieriksee: harbour gates into the Zuidhaven (left) and Noordhaven.

being easterly, were blowing from shelter and in the same direction as the tide, which always lessens the waves.

The Schelde in many ways resembles the estuarial Thames, save that the shipping can be more intense. At Terneuzen, where the canal from Gent debouches, the main channel lies close outside, and once again there is a tidal current that could set the unwary upon the entrance walls.

There are occasional patrol vessels at such points. They carry flashing lights, and their role is to shepherd the small craft when something enormous looms, such as a banana ship or an ore-carrier. As with many official boats, they have long periods with nothing to do; so they tend to rush over and tell you the rule of the road, the direction to Antwerp, and other things you probably knew already.

A 1,000-tonner from the Dortmund-Ems Canal clears Wemeldinge lock on her voyage southward.

Veere, in Zeeland. (left)

Pleasure boat moorings in the centre of Dordrecht. (facing page)

Leaving a Boat Abroad

In France it is difficult to leave your boat over the winter. There is little concept of such a thing; lock-keepers tend to shy away from the responsibility, and boatyards are few and far between. In Holland there are fewer problems, and although vandalism has risen from its previous low level in the big cities of 'the West', it is common in the country to see small boats tethered out on their own within plain view of a busy road.

Off the beaten track at, say, Oldeboorn, the local garage or friendly neighbours will keep an eye on a boat for several weeks, without mention of charge. You may moor in the town then, outside people's houses.

I left *Arthur* over one winter at Staveren, at a cost of £25 for six months, at the end of the old town canal outside the railway station. Since the station was unattended and people left their bicycles there all day, unlocked, it seemed safe enough. No-one touched the boat, save the lads from the shipyard, who moved *Arthur* a couple of times in order to shift other craft from the moorings there.

In the crowded south things can be harder. There is a tendency to wave the newcomer towards an expensive marina, and lock-keepers and other officials have become accustomed to doing this. I left *Arthur* in a marina at Hellevoetsluis in the south for one winter, literally wedged between two sets of piles. This is one of the problems of a comparatively beamy boat in a marina; there may not be room for you. With *Arthur* a Tom and Jerry situation evolved in which we had to charge the mooring full tilt in

order to get into it, the timber piles springing apart like tuning forks. Finding the marina expensive, I opted later for the small workboat harbour next door, a depository for tugs and hulks. There someone bashed the boat in my absence, bending one of the awning poles. In such a place one takes one's chance, and barges have the advantage. When I returned to Hellevoetsluis after four months away, a water official who lived nearby told me he had made it his business to keep his eye on *Arthur*, it being a 'poor part of the town'. In the light of my own experiences I would put the level of misdeeds there on a par with the Hebridean islands.

I recommend any visitor wishing to leave his boat in the Netherlands not to be browbeaten into using a disciplined marina, which can be very expensive at recent rates of exchange, but to ask around, heading if necessary for smaller canals in the country. The train service is just as good, and the enquirer after a berth for his craft will not be greeted with sullen stares and evasive replies. The Dutch, by and large, are very constructive, trusting and full of worthwhile suggestions.

It is also noteworthy that old town canals in spots such as Dordrecht and Sneek are properly used for local pleasure craft. While the visitor would be lucky indeed to acquire such a mooring in a larger town, I commend this practice to Britain's own authorities, with the comment that boat moorings bring life and interest to a community, that they take the pressure off the rest of the network, and that, if there are sufficient of them, their supervision and protection in these vandalistic times is scarcely expensive.

Buying a Barge : the Market

The family owned barge is a symbol of independence. She can be given a jolly name, and painted in bright colours. She may ply freely to a thousand places. Barges carry a certain placidity also; their pace is a natural one, the crews wave to one another as they pass.

Dutch barges, particularly, are invested with historical character. There are photographs taken at the turn of the century of sailing barges trapped in the ice, the captains posed before them. Old barges rarely die, and the same ones still trade today, motorized now but with sufficient trace of ancestry to connect them with the paintings of life under sail in the Zuyder Zee Museum at Enkhuizen.

The Dutch government has done its darndest to drive small motor barges from the system. Owners have received a generous pension if a vessel is cut up and fed into a crusher at the shipbreakers near Dordrecht, while the system of awarding cargoes has been adjusted and is less in favour of their operators. But the smaller vessels still work in trade: *klippers*, not unlike the *Cutty Sark* in hull form; *klipperaaks*, with an apple-cheeked back end; straight stemmed *steilstevens*; *paviljoentjalks, IJsseltjalks, hagenaars*. Some are rare indeed, unconverted, but you may bet, on learning of some early type that has disappeared or converted in its entirety into yachts, that a prime example will come stumping around a corner, like the Dodo, unexpectedly alive and well and living in Mauritius.

Inevitably, after a couple of years in the Netherlands I succumbed to the lure, and began looking for a Dutch barge

myself. The same sense of comfort that demanded a cabin stove in *Arthur* now required a wheelhouse. The Dutch waterways are unlike the French. They do not have frequent locks to engender healthy exercise, and can be long and windswept. There are times when you enjoy them better from behind glass, sitting down at a wheel, with some coffee at your elbow.

Barges in Amsterdam. (Hugh Potter)

A small klipper, *converted. Traditional craft of such a size are highly prized.*

One cold day on the Oude Maas, when my crew were disporting themselves below, laughing at their own jokes and occasionally beaming aft at me from the shelter of the hatchway, I realized that ours was the only vessel, of the hundred or so seen that afternoon, on which the steerer was compelled to stand upright at the tiller. I was developing the Leeds & Liverpool version of athlete's foot: I started to look in earnest at Dutch barges.

From out of the great mass of inland shipping, there are inevitably many vessels available second hand. They are advertised in dozens in the barge people's weekly newspaper *Schuttevaer*. Under the heading *Te Koop* (for sale) may be found *motortankschips*, 1,000 ton *Dortmunders*, and down at the other end of the scale, small *motorschips*. At the time I looked, these included one or two *klippers* of between 100 and 200 tons, a capacity just surviving in trade, while there were numerous yachts. Some of these were based on *botters*, the traditional fishing craft of the Zuyder Zee; more often on *tjalks*, one-time cargo vessels that are longer and more level in appearance. The *Schuttevaer* also carries advertisements for crew, steersmen and partners ready to share the operation of some trading vessel; but these require some understanding of Dutch. The 'for sale' situation, on the other hand, is well-nigh universal, and the advertisements are easily comprehended.

At a time when the prices of English narrow boats – which could carry 25 tons in their heyday – were soaring to a ridiculous level, it was astonishing to find that, for considerably less, 25,000 guilders, one could acquire a 200-ton motor barge. Such a vessel was advertised in the first issue of the *Schuttevaer* that I picked up. Her condition was said to be good, with a Mercedes diesel, recently overhauled, and new cabin accommodation aft. The hull was built in 1910, not the disadvantage it might seem, since materials were excellent and workmanship good in the period between 1895 and 1920, when the majority of these smaller 'ships' were built, while the standards of maintenance rival those of the most fastidious yachtsmen. On the Netherlands waterways barges are hosed down daily, painted continually, and the smallest dent is regarded as a disaster. Insurance is generally through barge-people's co-operatives, and craft are surveyed regularly and modified where necessary to conform to high standards. That insurance premiums stand at rock bottom confirms the enormous pride and skill with which most craft are handled.

The price of fl.25,000, as it is often expressed, is equivalent to just under £6,000 at the time of writing; but the impact on a Dutchman is not nearly as great. Within recent memory, ten guilders could be exchanged for £1. By 1971 it was eight guilders, and by 1973, when I first went to the Netherlands in *Arthur*, it was 6.3. The rate subsequently fell again to little over four guilders to the pound. It is this slide in Sterling that has made the price of goods appear so high in western Europe: high to Britons, but not to Continentals, an obvious point that seemed to escape some the participants in the debate on joining the EEC.

Thus the cost of this sample 200-tonner was little over that of the average motor car in the Netherlands, not bad for

Sailing tjalk *running before the wind near Elburg.*

a vessel over 100 feet long, with accommodation to rival a house. It was the higher price of fl.45,000 for an 80-ton *klipper* that gave some clue to the situation: there were many barges that were too small to yield a good living, and 200-tonners came into that category, but too big to be re-equipped as 'yachts'. And so, ironically, as the barges get smaller they become more valuable again.

There are further complications. Craft that can be converted back to sail are highly prized. There is a fashion for this, particularly at the IJsselmeer ports such as Enkhuizen, Hoorn or Staveren, where a holiday charter trade has developed on lines similar to that employing Thames sailing barges. Many Dutch trading craft, originally built for sailing and motorized later, convert back admirably to taking large parties, often of Germans, on sailing expeditions around the lake, or out to the Frisian Islands. Thus a *klipper*, with a flowing counter stern, is more valuable than a *klipperaak*, which is held to sail less sweetly. There are other motor barges, built as such from the outset, which are even cheaper, because they lack this sailing potential.

It was into this scene that I plunged.

The Search

The first encounter was a casual one in early summer, at the entrance to the Biesbos. There, beside one of the entry locks and under siege by ducklings, lay a small motor barge. The words *Te Koop* were roughly painted on the side.

The lock-keeper knew nothing of her save the address of the owner, who lived in a council house nearby and, inevitably, was out. I peered into the engineroom, a maze of pipes and taps, the paraphernalia of air-bottle starting, which I decided was beyond me. She was cluttered also with the derricks, bucket and heavy motor winch that signified a sand-dredger. She was not for me, but I liked the glimpses of varnished mahogany through the stern windows, suggestive of cosy cabins; and from then on I kept an eye cocked for others.

By the end of the season *Arthur* was lying in Staveren, and on a winter visit I travelled to Groningen to tramp its streets and gaze at barges. This, I reckoned, was the sort of place to look. There are many 'ships' in Friesland, and being remote from the capital and the fleshpots of 'the West', as Frieslanders so often term the cities beyond Amsterdam, it seemed likely that prices would be less. Broadly these surmises were correct, but a few preliminary enquiries and the odd haggle beside a decayed houseboat soon convinced me that I would be hopelessly out of my depth, bargaining in a foreign land.

It is unwise, in my opinion, to buy one of these vessels without the co-operation of a knowledgeable, helpful and honest Dutchman. By accident I met Jan de Jong, who ran a small yacht and barge brokerage from one of the cottages along Staveren's town canal. Whether I embroiled him, or he me, I am still uncertain. There were slight language difficulties; Jan's standard greeting of 'Hey, good-bye to you!' still rings in my ears, and on two subsequent occasions I had to travel out to Staveren to conduct a negotiation that in normal conditions might have been managed on the telephone. But Jan was energetic, and in a short time had come up with a list of barges. I went over again to look, staying on *Arthur* each night and chipping the ice from the washing-up bowl in the morning before walking round the shipyard to coffee at Jan's place.

There he would engage me further in barge lore. An old man would come to see him, with faded snaps of his *tjalk* crossing the IJsselmeer under sail. There would be photographs in Jan's collection of books and old brochures of the insurance syndicates, of captains standing proudly at their wheels, or gazing ruefully at the effects of a complete Rhine barge passing over the centre of their vessel. Outside,

A flashback to Cologne. Arthur's *steering position is uncomfortable on a hostile day. (facing page)*

Biblical decoration, Hindeloopen

Swing bridge between Bolsward and Sneek.

*Winter landscape in North Holland
near Alkmaar.* (Theo Kampa)

in the shipyard, the men would be welding and grinding as they had been doing from the early hours. The Dutch are tough and hardy. 'Blooming cold' I might growl. 'Oh, this is normal for the time of year.' Down the road at the café, where the old men used to sit around a big circular table, there were splendid canvas hangings on the wall, with scenes from battles and sleighs going across the ice, all browned by 'baccy-smoke and rubbed through at their edges by the impact of elbows and the backs of chairs. Once, while walking down the lonesome main street to the far end of the town, I heard a *chuckata-chuckata-chuckata*, and glimpsed above the far embankment the mast and wheel-house of a 500-tonner fairly storming out of the new town lock and into the IJsselmeer. This is barge country all right.

The men at the shipyard did not work on Sundays; nor did Jan. Then I would take my bicycle and pedal off to the distant horizon, toiling against the constant breezes as far as Hindeloopen, where an Allied bomber crew lies buried in the churchyard, or to the water town of Balk. In silhouette against the grey, flat light I would slowly tread the pedals on the long road back, as the fortified farmhouses, the spare distant trees, conjured up the tone of long-gone times. It is common today to project almost every land as a sunny holiday dream. Friesland has a different kind of magic.

Like many Dutchmen in the region, Jan had a car that ran on natural gas, obtained from wells near Groningen and rechargeable from a large missile casing at the local garage. Our morning sorties would begin with a trot behind the car, hands pressed against its chilly, unco-operative surfaces. This would precede a telephone call to the local dealer; then we would have more coffee, before the car finally decided to start. After that we would go to look at barges.

These varied, and Jan's shortlist ran the gamut of possibilities. Thirteen thousand guilders could buy a 180-tonner with a good engine, but her accommodation had been burned out in a fire. A little more money was asked for Jan's own *klipper*, the *Spes*, moored just outside. She had a nice 27

metre hull, and an adequate engine, but once again the accommodation had been gutted, in this case by Jan himself in pursuit of several fantasies of design. The local fetish for recreating sailing *klippers* involves much butchery around the after end, including hacking away the cabin and relocating the wheel in a heroic position at the stern. The *Spes* promised a lot of work, while her transmission system had double clutches to isolate a crash-type gearbox, and this looked cumbersome. Such arrangements are common among smaller barges in regular trades, where runs are steady and few engine movements are needed. In the canals of France, to which I hoped to return, there are many locks and each involves putting the engine in and out of gear perhaps a dozen times. A stout transmission system is vital.

Another important aspect of the French canals is the limited clearance at several points. I particularly looked forward to returning to the Canal du Nivernais, right in the heart of the French system, where the final flight of locks up to the summit, and those down to Cercy-la-Tour, are shorter than normal. The maximum possible length is around 30 metres and the maximum beam a whisker over 5 metres.

In the Netherlands sizes are not so critical. There are small waterways, it is true, but there is usually an alternative route, so that craft are of all manner of lengths, while the common standard of width at bridges and the like is a generous 6 metres. Craft have been built to 5.20, 5.30 and 5.50 metres, and the vendors are not always fussy. This I found with the next barge I looked at, a small *luxe motor*. These are straight-stemmed vessels, usually with the wheelhouse forward of the accommodation, and one of the first types to be specifically built with an engine rather than as a sailing vessel or a sailing auxiliary.

This ship had 'spread', that is to say expanded, through carrying scrap iron without the tie-bars in place across the hold. Scrap and cement are among the most damaging cargoes, the cement attacking the plates and frames, the scrap distorting the hull through being dropped and wrenched by cranes. Her owner swore to me as a Dutchman that his barge was exactly 5 metres in beam, and this was a great pity. I managed to measure her when he was not looking, using a tape from a point on the centreline of the hatches, to a vertical established by Jan holding a boathook against each side in turn. She was about 5 metres and 30 centimetres across. As further evidence, a large slab-like vessel had moored alongside, and the bulge of one hull was marked against the straightness of the other. The *luxe motor's* engineroom was a maze of rusty pipes, extending like creeper from a big three-cylinder Deutz. Fortunately the owner was such a good salesman that he had forgotten to charge up the air bottle to start the engine, and that was the end of it.

First view of Secunda, *sandwiched against the dock wall in Rotterdam.*

One other that I looked at was a 200-tonner with a big modern Kromhout, an excellent diesel of 145 hp, which yielded the terrifying speed of 25 kilometres per hour, around 14 knots, when the ship was unladen. She had electric steering as well, and was for sale at only 18,000 guilders; but she was too long, with a deep hull that would be difficult to convert. Michael Streat who was with me at the time liked her a lot, perhaps because she had a bridge just forward of the wheelhouse, from which he could do Charles Laughton imitations. In so doing he bashed his head on the overhanging roof, and was deterred.

I looked at three other Dutch barges back in England. One was good, but with the wheelhouse right aft. Since the idea was growing that we would convert the barge into a 'hotel ship', some sort of separation between guests and crew seemed mutually beneficial, so a forward wheelhouse was called for. The other two, once beautiful craft, were run down and dirty with sagging cabin linings in the accommodation. Their price was tempting but I knew how much toil is involved in working up a vessel of that size.

Patience was wearing a little thin when Jan and I set off for Rotterdam to look at *Secunda*. It was yet another icy morning; getting out of bed had been harder than usual, and we had delayed twice to extract middle-aged gentlemen from upturned cars on the road between Lemmer and Emmeloord. Fortunately Jan had practised on a skidpan, or we might have suffered the same fate.

The *Secunda* lay in one of the Rotterdam docks, waiting to load coffee for a short-haul run to Utrecht. She was a *klipper*, with a hooked bow and overhanging stern. There was modern-looking accommodation aft of the wheelhouse. This had greatly impressed Jan on an exploratory visit. 'So big and clean. All painted. You can see there have been vimmin on this ship.' A chill wind lashed around the moorings as we climbed aboard.

She was certainly the smartest I had seen at that time, a vessel in the proud tradition of working barges rather than a

faded example that had fallen on harder times. Paint can cover a multitude of sins, but a vessel like this, still working, speaks of pride in ownership. That was my first impression on walking aft to meet the Mudde family.

Mr and Mrs Mudde lived in organized comfort. The wheelhouse, which I later discovered had never been folded down during their ownership, was fitted out as a dining room. It had a carpet, a refrigerator, and a jungle of potted plants. Mr Mudde, who was so tall that he could not properly stand in this area, sat in a corner when steering. With one hand on the wheel he would stoop down when it was raining to peer like Chad through the small arc of a tiny windscreen wiper. He gave me a demonstration at our berth.

The wheel itself was a beautifully assembled piece of woodwork, about a metre in diameter, with an outer rim of bent ash. There were two control levers alongside, for throttle and gears, forward, neutral and astern; also a wheel for controlling engine temperature, and a bevy of porcelain fuses. This corner, and the engineroom beneath, were Mr Mudde's province; the remainder was his wife's. The aft accommodation was a world of carpets, lace curtains, plants and wedding photographs. Behind the stove was a sheet of imitation brickwork, printed onto asbestos; above it, on the wallpaper, flew a trio of ducks, moulded out of pottery.

This saloon extended almost the whole width of the ship. Forward of it lay a small galley and washing facilities; aft, two sleeping cabins. We had coffee, Mrs Mudde having laid out a table which, I realized, had its legs carefully adjusted to present a horizontal surface, whereas the floor tilted slightly. The ceiling too had a considerable rake, introduced entirely for aesthetic purposes. Mrs Mudde, who was short in stature, could move freely, whereas her husband and son, another giant, had only certain regions they could occupy. Later I was to see why all the bunks, including some nominal singles, were built so wide. It was to enable those of beanpole stature to sleep on the diagonal, since the bunks were less than six feet long.

We looked into the engineroom, clambering down through a steel hatch bearing a Donald Duck transfer, distributed by some oil company, and past a fierce notice telling people not to smoke or strike matches. A smartly painted Gardner diesel held sway, one of the best British makes. Its gearbox was absent, and replaced by a German Reintjes : one of the best again, they hastily assured me. The propeller shaft ran aft a long way, between the overlapping riveted plates of the fine-lined stern. There was a small generator on the far side, which Mr Mudde Jnr started with a casual flip of the arm.

Then we looked at the forecabin, presently in use as the ship's laundry, and I measured the width of the hull, which corresponded within a centimetre to the dimensions listed in

Mrs Mudde tends the washing. At this time the bow cabin was in use as the ship's laundry.

the ship's papers. These, the *Meetbrief* and *Certificaat van Onderzoek*, are most important in any purchase, confirming when the vessel was built, her salient dimensions, and her authorization to trade. They also contain tables showing the trim and displacement of the ship at various stages of loading, set against marks cut into the hull side. These are most valuable in considering trim and flotation during ballasting or conversion.

Over more coffee, we discussed the world in general, direct haggling being difficult. Neither of the Mudde parents spoke English, the son only a little; but gradually the basic facts of the vessel emerged. She had been built in 1900, at Papendrecht, just across the water from Dordrecht, as a sailing vessel. At various times she had been altered, her side decks raised for more cargo capacity, her masts removed. While down in the hold, a great barn under a timber tent of hatch covers, Mr Mudde had pointed out where the chainplates had once been fastened to receive the rigging, and how she had apparently been lengthened, a common practice in Holland although this must have been accomplished many years ago for the riveting was quite uniform and the hull material unchanged. For a long time now construction in Holland has been by welding, and the types of steel employed have gradually altered.

There had apparently been another rebuild in the 1960s, when the Gardner was installed and the new wheelhouse and aft accommodation added. The Muddes had owned *Secunda* for five years, and prior to that, as I later discovered, there had been a period of hard working and a little neglect, for there were signs of corrosion around the winch on the foredeck. When I came to know *Secunda* better, I discovered all manner of signs of the work that the Mudde family had put into her. The cargo hatch coamings had been stripped from end to end with a rotary sander and repainted with many coats, like a Rolls Royce; the entire engineroom had been prettied up; in the wheelhouse and companionway every scrap of varnish gleamed. They had had her surveyed twice, it being a condition of the insurance co-operative to which they belonged that the vessel be examined every three years. It is a pleasant illustration of the bargeing attitude that the insurers waited until you reported an accident before they checked that you had complied.

The asking price was in the region of 30,000 guilders, with room for haggling about engine spares, household effects, and the fact that the Muddes wanted to go on using *Secunda* for three more months, before their new ship *Gazelle* would be ready. This was apparently a bigger, beamier vessel – the Muddes never worked out of the Netherlands – and they would be moving onto her at the yard in Staveren.

With memories of the car trade, I pondered taking the vessel for a spin, or at least suggesting that we might do so, but frankly I found the view down over the hatches to the distant bow rather daunting, and wondered whether I could get such a vessel through the narrow entrance of the dock. It seemed to be taken for granted on all sides that barges travelled reasonably and that handling them was just a matter of course. I was happy to comply, and contented myself with hearing the engine running. Jan and I then departed, for Friesland and a period of reflection.

Mr Mudde explains the switchgear and controls.

The Legalities

Several telephone calls, a fistful of letters and a personal visit later, I decided to purchase *Secunda*. Another buyer was said to be in the offing, so Jan wanted some money to secure the deal. I went to my bank in London to arrange the transfer. Speed was the essence: Sterling was falling rapidly, the recession was getting under way. I had been declared 'redundant' in my recently-acquired job, and while this gave me a useful sum of money there was little prospect of more save through freelance writing, a precarious occupation.

There was a matter of an import licence, so the bank assured me. There was not: several days later I discovered that I merely had to write O.G.I.L. (Open General Import Licence) on the form, and Bank of England permission had then been obtained. Jan wanted to pay the money over, and with traditional British scepticism I decided to send him a deposit; but the forms that the bank had given me made no provision for such a thing. In the cosy world of the person who drew them up, you received your goods first, as a parcel upon your doorstep, and *then* paid for them. Meanwhile Sterling was falling like a lift on which the cables had snapped. While all this dithering was going on, my wealth was disappearing before my eyes.

I made two applications for currency transfer, one for a ten per cent deposit to be sent out to Jan straight away, while the residue was to follow. In the event the second sum arrived in Staveren before the first; but in the meantime Jan had lost patience and put down a deposit from his own

money. He also arranged the legal transfer of *Secunda* through a Dutch solicitor, cautioning that as soon as the deal was completed I had three months to take the vessel out of the Netherlands before paying Dutch Value Added Tax, which then stood at 16 per cent.

There were two other complications. The first was

Secunda, Arthur and a Dutch yacht, together in the outer harbour at Staveren. A ketch-rigged klipper lies astern.

insurance. It is extremely difficult to get cover for a Continental barge. Many of the established insurance companies in Britain, happy as they are to enrol all manner of fibreglass cockleshells, will not touch barges. They know little about them, and seem surprised that anything so old can stay afloat a minute longer. But through a friend in the trade I found a broker who got me quotes at Lloyds, of seven, five, and finally of one-and-a-half per cent premium for the single trip to Calais, and then to England. This cover was conditional on the last surveyor's report, which Jan and I drove to Heerenveen to obtain. Later I was to find a sympathetic, if proper, broker on the normal pleasure-boat market, but all these procedures can be tiresome, not to say trying for those to whom time is as short as cash, and are reduced to bellowing, long-distance phone calls from a windswept box stuck on a wall.

The second complication came as a bombshell. 'Yachting' suddenly became subject to a new luxury rate of British Value Added Tax, at 25 per cent of the estimated value of craft bought or imported. It was quite impossible to get *Secunda* to England before the deadline, and I had not got the money to pay. There was hope of exemption because *Secunda* was a cargo vessel, but in the chaos and ambiguities of a taxation system having different rates for 'safety equipment' and sundry classifications that escaped the net, it was impossible to be sure. Again, one needs time, money and/or a good solicitor. I managed without, although the remaining hairs fell from the top of my head, and established that VAT would not be levied, provided that the ship was over 15 tons in displacement and was not converted for 'recreation or pleasure'. It was an intriguing use of the word 'or', but a great relief. These aspects of the tax became more widely known later, but they weren't then; and subsequently this high rate of VAT was rescinded, though not before many small boatyards were forced into bankruptcy. And even now arguments rage as to whether a lamp, for instance, is used to signify being at anchor ('safety') or to light up a cabin ('luxury').

Barge Handling

There are lots of *Secundas* in the Netherlands, where a handful of names are used over and over again, also *Vertrouwen* ('Trusty'), *Rival* ('Breadwinner'), *Voorwaards* or the Biblical *Eben-haezer*. My own *Secunda* had been based at Lekkerkerk, a small township on the Lek, and bore a signboard to this effect, while the name 'the second one', or 'the one that follows', was appropriate as the successor to *Arthur*. The nameboard looked good as I viewed her from across the outer harbour of Staveren, and realized she was mine.

She was trimmed slightly by the stern, Jan having loaded her with 30 tons of gravel. There are many barge pundits in Staveren, and it was their combined and considered opinion that *Secunda* would handle better with such a load. Accordingly Jan had nailed some old hatch covers to the timber floor of the hold, to act as shuttering should the ship roll. He had then taken her to a nearby wharf and loaded aboard the gravel.

So awed was I by this massive vessel that I had decided to wait for absolute calm before attempting even the most elementary manoeuvres. I had seen how barges could be carried sideways on the wind, and how the steersmen and women needed the courage of their convictions. Briskness and confidence would be called for, but I definitely needed practice. With a small crew from England, I settled down like Jerome's Captain Goyles, to wait for the weather.

I had struck up a rudimentary acquaintance with an old man with a peaked cap and only one ear, who used to come

and spit in the harbour, and confide in me in thick Frisian. He had a beautiful *klipper* himself, somewhat smaller than *Secunda*. I had seen her up on the slipway in the town canal, a vessel all the more intriguing in that she had no engine.

One day she appeared in the outer harbour, borne on the howling wind, and propelled by a small steel dinghy with a pop-pop diesel. Since the dinghy was lashed under the

Philip Streat at the wheel, with Arthur *in tow.*

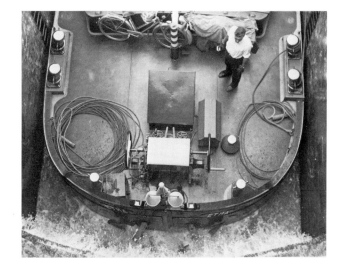

The bluff bow and foredeck of a spits.

stern, the master of the smaller craft could see very little and was obliged to receive instructions from an elderly trio who rushed about the *klipper*'s deck and screeched at him. After several encores these would penetrate his balaclava helmet and some juggling with levers would follow. The engine would falter momentarily and the ensemble changed direction. Miraculously they slowed their convoy down, within feet of us, spun the whole lot around and nestled into a vacant berth. Much impressed, I asked Jan who they were. 'Oh,' he said, 'they are three old men and their sister. Two are old enough now to be paid by the Government [meaning that they received a pension], the rest they have to go on vorking. They have this ship small enough to go up the little canals, so they have, what do you call it, a mono-poley?'

Apparently they thought nothing of sailing out into the IJsselmeer, fully loaded, with this two-boat arrangement, and it was common for them to voyage to Amsterdam. Inspired by this example, we reckoned we should do something ourselves; a spin on the IJsselmeer, to be

followed by a leisurely journey through Friesland and inside the polders to Amsterdam, with a direct return to Staveren across the lake. Then, with *Arthur* in tow, we would set out again, for England.

Stopping is the biggest problem in handling any boat or ship. Space to manoeuvre is what the helmsman requires. Before our first voyage, I sent a scout to check that nothing was entering the outer harbour, for the narrows between the moles were concealed from view. That being clear, we cast off all ropes and let the ship drift a foot or so clear from the wall. I put the wheel over and a brief touch in forward gear sent the stern back in towards the wooden piles and the bow further out. With the stern still rubbing the piles I repeated this manoeuvre, to lever the bow out even further. Then, with the wheel over in the other direction, a further short burst took the stern out too, so that we were now well clear of the wall and unlikely to scrape along it. Pivoting just forward of a central point, *Secunda* straightened up, and with nothing ahead we could motor straight out.

The chart of the IJsselmeer showed deep water all the way to an outer buoy, about three kilometres to the southwest. Farther down the coast lay the Vrouwezand, the Woman's Sand. In its approach to this bank, such swell as remained upon the lake was becoming markedly steeper. This provided my first insight into Dutch motor barges in open water: they roll. Hastily we took her from the broadside position, headed into the swell and cleared up some broken crockery.

Next I tried to gauge her stopping power near the buoy. Most vessels swing one way or the other when going hard astern; this is the paddlewheel effect, so called because the propeller acts like a paddle of the Mississippian type and trundles the stern sideways. *Secunda* had a left-handed propeller so that, with the engine in reverse gear – going astern to the nautical purist – the stern would swing to starboard, the bow to port. It was useful to know.

Our next experiment was with the bow rudder. This is a

device fitted to many Continental barges, for use when travelling unladen. The rudder lies in a vertical slot under the bow, and can be lowered by releasing a small winch on the foredeck. The rudder shaft runs upward through a long tube within the barge, and by fitting a tiller over the squared end of the shaft the bow can be manoeuvred. So runs the theory, and certainly I have seen many craft managed in this way, sometimes directly from the foredeck, occasionally by means of reins leading aft to the wheel-house. We fitted our own tiller and tried. The principle seemed easy enough; the results were chaotic. It seemed impossible to deflect the bow in the way intended; rather the rudder acted as a brake. We tried many combinations of speed and angle, but never with coherent results. The rudder was winched back into its slot, and we decided to do without. I tried it several times subsequently, but never got any sense from it. Perhaps ours was a bad one.

By passing near a buoy, and also by looking at the wash, we were beginning to gauge *Secunda*'s stopping power. With trepidation we then returned to the harbour. There was room to spare, so with the paddle-wheel effect firmly in mind we were able to turn, point to the free space at the quay and slow to a crawl before reaching it. Going astern again caused the bow to swing clear as it neared the wooden piling, so that we were able to glide alongside quite smoothly.

With confidence found, and the longer trip in prospect, I started purchasing: pots, pans and crockery for the ten friends who would be coming as far as Belgium; flags, engine oil, rope, rope, and more rope for the whole journey. Few ships ever have quite enough rope, and

experience with the Staveren bollards, distant blobs against the skyline, indicated that we would need it in mighty lengths for mooring, quite apart from the towing we proposed. I bought more charts, spare bulbs, grease, and a deck brush. The Dutch do not use grill-pans we discovered, perhaps that was why the one at Nijmegen came into the 'antique' category. I borrowed one from *Arthur*.

The high tradition of barge handling. Paddle tug and barge pass in the current at Pfalz, River Rhine. (Raab Karcher GmbH)

A Bigger Voyage

The seventeenth century brick watergate at Sneek.

Frisian boatyard.

Fortunately the lock at Staveren is long and wide, sufficiently so for the inexperienced to enter without striking the gates or abutments. The lock-keeper was solicitous, and helped us top up the water tank. This was of two tons capacity, in striking contrast to *Arthur*'s little canister. Thereafter we had a clear run all the way to Sneek, save for a few lift bridges. At these the technique was to sound the klaxon, giving a long blast to distinguish ourselves from passing cars, and glide to a crawl with plenty of space to spare. A cross-wind had developed as we approached our first; we needed all of the 300 metres or so we had allowed in which to motor forward and take *Secunda* back to the centre channel each time she blew aside. I was just contemplating leaning her against a flimsy timber staging, with all the delicacy I could muster, when the bridge lights turned to green and the span was lifted.

In Sneek conditions were even tighter. We could not afford to be windblown, since we found ourselves skimming down a narrow channel with fragile houseboats moored on each side. At the end, as I saw from the *waterkaart*, there was a lift bridge, and I doubted that this would be manned at so late an hour. I surreptitiously laid out tyres should we have to stop with only the surrounding boats to nestle against, but the Gods smiled again and around the final corner we found a barge length of clear space just before the bridge. It is for such arrivals that spaces like this are kept clear.

In the morning, I knew, we would have to negotiate the bridge and the tight right-angled turn that immediately

Secunda *at Enkhuizen*

Several klippers *have been converted back to sail, for charter on the IJsselmeer and Waddenzee.*

followed. With Philip Streat, Michael's son, I had planned the operation in advance, spotting a bollard we could pull against, and laying out a rope for this purpose. When the time came, we eased *Secunda* through the gap, and brought her to a halt just beyond, by means of the rope. We let out a fraction more, easing forward until her bow overhung the towpath ahead; then with the rudder over and the propeller turning slowly, she pivoted around and turned into the next canal.

Taking your time is a maxim in barge handling. Another important point we had noted was the necessity of being absolutely systematic with our ropes. Barge crews lay them down in big coils, always working away from a fixed end, always coiling in the same direction, which with normal rope is clockwise. We started apeing them, soon enough realizing that the forces involved on craft of this size are very powerful, and that a tangle can be disastrous.

Barges have big stub bollards, with cleat points on them. Although these bollards are arranged in pairs, both at the bow and beside the wheelhouse, they are not customarily used for receiving figure-of-eight turns. This is yachting practice, and indeed we had done the same on *Arthur*, which by comparison was also a small, light vessel, but the method does not develop as much friction as winding the rope round and round the same bollard.

So used to these methods did we become that both Philip and I developed a spontaneous cringe whenever our later crews did things differently.

Barges in Rough Water

By the time *Secunda* approached Amsterdam we had become practised enough to tuck her into the Oranjesluizen and under the stern of a 1,500-tonner without a qualm. By then we had realized that *Secunda* was a small ship; but the helmsmen of the big barges would also move their craft with aplomb, sitting in upholstered chairs and merely pressing buttons to make their wheels spin this way or that. I watched a crew of a 1,000-ton Dortmunder, real boyoes, bring their ship to a halt within millimetres of the wall, with time to wave and whistle at the girls as well. They had come directly across the IJsselmeer on a drenching, blowy day, deeply loaded. We had travelled inside the polder, with only the final more exposed section past Pampseiland to deal with. *Secunda*'s stern had twitched a little under the following breeze, but the waves here were comparatively small. Beyond Enkhuizen they would have been larger, with a stretch of water the width of the English Channel in which to get up steam. How, I wondered, had these other barges fared.

We gained some inkling on the journey back to Staveren, which we made directly across the IJsselmeer and into a strong headwind. *Secunda* began to pitch and bash. Spray started to fly, to be blown back in sheets across the hatches. Our steel dinghy, always something of a horror to secure, began to work to and fro at its lashings. An emergency party went aft to add more lines. With Marken lighthouse glinting in a baleful sun, we pushed forward to the lock at Enkhuizen, the new polder wall providing shelter.

Secunda *and* Arthur, *lashed side-by-side and flying a blue flag, being overtaken and passed on the River IJssel.*

Beyond here the waves had white tops on them, and were short and steep. *Secunda* shuddered occasionally, but made steady progress. Provided the seas came from directly ahead she just smashed through them, but at anything more than ten degrees off this course she began to roll and blow off sideways. Steering a compass course under such conditions is quite misleading, for there could be a sideways component in the equation. The only safe course, it seemed to me, was directly to windward, until shelter was gained.

Fortunately Staveren lay in that direction, so that the only cross-wind part of the journey was within the last few metres, after turning to face the harbour entrance. We got into line, keeping away from the pier end a little, and then took her in. As if to demonstrate the trouble we had avoided, *Secunda* gave a couple of sharp rolls as we moved into the calm of the harbour.

Towing

Empty barges often tow side-by-side, for reasons both social and economic. Only one need be motoring; the other is pulled on a line to her stern from a point near the bow of the tug. Breast ropes prevent the two from swinging apart.

We decided to tow *Arthur* back towards England in this fashion. We would separate the two where necessary, either on a long line, or with *Arthur* travelling independently for the occasional lock; but by towing for much of the time we would save fuel and aid progress, *Secunda* being significantly the faster. I duly bought two red flags with white squares at their centres, the accepted symbol for towing in the Netherlands.

In the early stages, when crossing some of the breezy Friesland meers, it seemed wiser to tow on a long line, to avoid damage if the vessels worked against one another. On my new ship a sizeable crowd, including a strong contingent from *Practical Boat Owner* magazine, would drink coffee in the comfort of the wheelhouse and look back at Michael Streat, who had bought *Arthur* from me, braced against the elements.

Both he and Rob, his crew, wore high-buttoned coats in a sort of cockroach colour, so that they seemed to be swathed in tarpaulin. Rob had evolved a system of chalking messages on a blackboard, which we could read through binoculars. In the estuaries south of Dordrecht, where we encountered driving winds with rain and spray, the messages were generally simple. They merely said 'How long?'

But through many of the wide canals, and on the arduous slog up the IJssel, we travelled side-by-side, hopping from one ship to the other at will, occasionally checking the chafe on the tyre fenders as *Arthur* bobbed in the wash of passing barges. Despite *Secunda*'s comparative agility, we were the slowest combination on the river. Everything overtook us, even an elderly barge loaded with scrap iron I had observed the previous evening at Zutphen, with a crowd of children on board watching their Dad erect the TV aerial. They only just had the legs on us, though, and crawled past against the streaming current, at one time bunching close alongside as we squeezed past a brace of downcomers.

Manoeuvring two breasted-up barges into a lock or against a quay requires a little concentration. When one slows down, the other will carry on, resulting in a sideways slide. I recalled this from narrow boat days in England. With working narrow boats, travelling as a pair, the unpowered boat, the butty, is always placed on the side nearer the bank for mooring. When they are headed into the bank and the engine is put astern, the butty continues and slews them neatly alongside.

We got into Willemstad locks like this, just ahead of a Belgian 1,000-tonner which came slamming in full tilt. Her owner, nattily attired in leather trilby, brought her to a stand by flicking a wire hawser onto a bollard, then putting some turns on the bitts at the bow. While he was doing this, he looked over his shoulder and shouted a few *bons mots* at the keeper.

In the confusion of craft pressing to get into the Zuid

TOWING

Beveland Canal, it was necessary to make our separate ways in the queue. *Secunda* filled the triangle of space at the back of the lock, behind several large barges that had entered first. I had thought there was insufficient room for us alone, but the loudspeaker called *Arthur* forward also, to fit in the triangle left by ourselves.

From then on it was the long line and blackboard again, down the Schelde and into Belgium.

The approaches to Bruges, with double-manned liftbridge in the background.

A Route through Belgium

The route taken by *Arthur* and *Secunda* through Belgium is of interest, in that it shortens the sea passage to or from England. Free from the worries of sandbanks and appalling Force eights, it offers a safe and entertaining journey for those who are not essentially sea-doggy.

At Terneuzen, the last Netherlands lock before the frontier, the traveller in a barge is plied with incomprehensible forms, printed in Dutch only. One may fill these in as one wishes; certainly the man who collects them doesn't bother to read the replies.

From Terneuzen to Gent the route is along a wide, straight ship canal, lined with heavy industry. Whenever a big ship appears police launches fuss around it, to keep pleasure craft and *spits* out of the propellers. The 350 ton *spits* or *péniche* type is a popular breed in Belgium, where it is often handled with speed and cheek. In Belgium it is far less likely that a *péniche* will slow down when passing a mooring, and fast-revving powerful diesel engines are all the rage.

Part way up the Ship Canal is Sas van Gent, the frontier. There is nominally a lock and barrage, but the whole lot were open and many vessels were not bothering to stop. We did, and had a difficult time in finding anyone to take an interest in us. The only person on the alert was a lad sitting on a camp stool in the whirlwind eddying around the corner of the Customs house. His job was compiling statistics and plainly he was not elevated enough to be allowed inside.

I had to coerce a man into stamping all Jan de Jong's forms, but it was fortunate that I did so, as the authorities chased Jan three months later in search of revenue, or proof that we had exported. Since none of the occupants of the frontier office came out to check the vessels they were certifying, we could have exported a whole fleet.

In Belgium our red and white flags took on a different meaning. One of these must be flown at the bow of every craft under way, or wishing to make progress. This sorts out those waiting for a lock from those who have tied up for the duration, a useful and sensible guide. Lock-keepers often insist that yachts not flying such a flag should promptly do so. It is well to be so provided.

Gent itself now has a ring canal. The intricate old waterways at its centre, once a bottleneck from which boat-owners emerged several days later prematurely aged and gibbering, have been converted into roads. There is a new lock on the ring, a dreary place, where they ask why you have no permit. These cost ten Belgian francs for *Secunda* (about 12½ pence at the time) and five francs for *Arthur*. We were taken into the lavatorial tiled office with a resigned air, and issued with the permits there.

Those with memories of the dying days of English narrow boat traffic will find many similarities on the canal route to Bruges, a decayed canal, largely in a cutting, along which the occasional *péniche* thrashes mercilessly, visibly destroying the banks. Still persisting in travelling side-by-side, in a canal that was subtly becoming narrower, we had a narrow escape just before a hairpin bend, around which a succession of small empty barges came shooting, flat-out, without warning or slowing down. We decided thereafter to proceed in line.

Mistakenly, as it proved, we moored *Secunda* for the night to an iron bollard and a solid granite milepost, set deeply into the ground. At 5.30 a.m. a loaded *péniche* hurtled past, there was a loud bang, and we broke loose. The line itself was intact, but the stone was nowhere to be found. Nor were there marks in the ground; it must have been projected like some medieval missile, Heaven knows where.

There are numerous lift bridges along this section, worked by two men, one each side of the canal. Each bridge ascends between two towers, and if one man winds his handle faster than the other, it does so crookedly. Travelling towards Bruges in the early morning we encountered hordes of working people, crowding the water's edge as they waited for each bridge to be lowered again. I would willingly have let them cross first, particularly in one case where the factory hooter was blowing; but the keepers would have none of it and stolidly wound away. Had we gone into the side, I believe we might have been lynched.

Gradually, as Bruges is approached, there is a strong smell, resulting from the local attitude to drains. The old canal through the city, the Coupure, is black with sewage, and it is remarkable that this otherwise splendid place, so dependent on tourism, is not regularly swept by plague. The Coupure, though closed to through traffic, affords useful moorings at either end. The smell apart, Bruges is superb, and there is an impressive view from the famous belfry, ascended by almost 400 steps. A man climbs these regularly with an oilcan, to tend the carillon that strikes for so long that the time between the quarters is largely occupied by reverberation.

The entrance to the old city canal, the Coupure, provides a convenient refuge at Bruges.

The Begijnhof in Bruges

Despite quite heavy traffic, the ring canal at Bruges embodies an ancient circular lock, unique in its complexity. A side exit from the chamber leads through double gates into the Canal de Damme, which is on an intermediate level. Barge captains wishing to pass through it can only do so if they are moored at that side of the lock. Since they invariably arrive in a different order, there is much running up and down the arterial road as middle-aged *batelliers* and choleric lock-keepers strive to exchange messages above the din of pulsating vehicles. Over each lock exit is a lift-bridge, guaranteed to paralyse the traffic, and there is a permit office facing in the opposite direction. It is a feature of all such offices along this route that those inside cannot see the subject under discussion. Boat owners become quite good at describing the main features of their vessels.

Having filled their circular lock with a variety of craft, and caused a great delay on the roadway, by letting a couple of *péniches* into the Canal de Damme, the keepers at Bruges lapsed into a state of catalepsy and nothing happened at all for a further half hour. Perhaps the interval is mandatory, to let the traffic settle down again before the next upheaval; perhaps the keepers were merely gathering strength for the final hysterical onslaught. In the flurry of activity that suddenly broke the calm, gestures and counter-commands were freely exchanged, whistles were blown, and *Arthur* cannoned into the bow of an elderly 500-tonner called *Gilbert*, both having been told to leave at the same time.

Such sizeable craft continue to ply along the canal to Ostende, their wash cascading along the banks. It is an attractive route in parts, with vistas of leaning trees stark in the beautiful Belgian light, and white swing bridges that lend themselves to reflection. Plasschendale lock, a large gated oval, provides access to the next canal, the Canal de Plasschendale itself, which leads to Nieupoort. There is an awkward railway bridge a short way along it, well supplied with thunderous expresses, and there can be a long wait.

The horrifying battles of Ypres were fought just to the south, and there is plenty of evidence in the area, with trenches and spoiled ground still discernible. At Nieupoort, three waterways connect through locks formally arranged around the head of the tidal passage from the sea, and we found strong eddies in these, making the crossing difficult. A large memorial to King Albert dominates the scene, and there is a permit-stamping office hidden among the formal gardens. Just outside the town a new lock provides access to the River Yser, and may well be the preferred route in the years to come.

The Canal de Furnes leads away from the complex on the far side. Furnes itself, though badly hit in both World Wars, has managed to escape the cemented blight that followed. Its gabled square is still complete, and there is a calm little basin

Lock, now closed, on the Coupure.

for mooring. Before it is a succession of swing bridges, all on bends. At one such, television cameras prevent the operator from lowering the structure upon vessels which, inevitably, he cannot see. For those delayed here, and out of sight around the preceding bend, a notice in Flemish refers to a sort of bird-box containing a telephone.

Furnes lock is the last depository for permits; beyond that, beside the main road at Ghyvelde, stands the frontier. Examination here is normally cursory, although we found it impossible to obtain a French Green Card, still the accepted means of establishing entry, as they had not got any. This attracted some interesting pronouncements later, when

Damme Canal

trying to leave France, which we were prevented from doing for some time on the grounds that we had not officially entered.

A further peculiarity of the French portion of the Canal de Furnes is that it has fallen into such a state of disrepair that a one-way system is enforced over a short stretch. The restriction is firmly applied despite the negligible traffic. If you arrive fifteen minutes after time, as we did, it is necessary to wait nearly four hours before negotiating two swing bridges and the short length between them. No amount of fulminating or hinting at bribes will do any good; the resolution and determination of French keepers to stick to the rules is one of the wonders of the European system.

The Canal de Furnes, a little-used drain, sidles into Dunkerque by the back door. There are some very low bridges along it, nominally of 3.50 metres clearance although we found 3.80 metres due to a deliberate lowering of the level in order to drain off heavy rainfall from the fields. Both in size and character, this waterway resembles the Nene above Wisbech, or the Trent and Mersey near Burton. Neither sets the scalp tingling, unless you have a 3.70 metre wheelhouse like *Secunda*'s. The technique at doubtful bridges is to stop before them, sidle up until the high spot on the ship is practically touching, and if there is little more than a rivet-head's thickness involved, to open up the throttle savagely. The stern will then sink as much as six inches as the vessel drives through. A nuance of the operation is to look both ahead and astern first, to check that no long shallow wave is approaching from some distant lock or oncoming vessel. Such waves, just distinguishable by a change of reflection on a calm day, may raise the level by that vital six inches, and the manoeuvre can be disastrously undone.

A deep lock admits the voyager to Dunkerque, which is horrible. When passing through with *Arthur* and *Secunda* there was a torrential downpour, and this seemed quite appropriate. Many trading craft are laid up here, among a complex of traffic islands. Decrepit vessels laden with sawdust come sidling in from the docks, while stinking water and boatmen in old army greatcoats complete the picture.

There is a choice of routes to Calais. One is through the Canal de Bourbourg, another small waterway; the other is down the new Liason, the direct route into the interior from the Dunkerque docks. By comparison with the Bourbourg's two, this has one lock only, a large concrete affair like a flooded prisoner-of-war camp. Both these waterways connect with the lovely River Aa, a narrow stream lined with poplars, usually seen in flat grey light and reminiscent of early photographs. The Canal de Calais leads off, rural and pleasant, although I was distressed to see that the tall elm trees that overhung the approaches to the lock at Henuin had become diseased and been felled. Without them this little hamlet loses much of its charm.

At Calais lies the lowest bridge on the route from Paris, but *Secunda* again squeezed under by our opening up the throttle. There followed a basin and a lock into the Bassin Carnot, which is part of the docks complex. Here particulars are always sought again, and those who have got into the country without evidence of doing so are sent off to the Customs Bureau. This is equidistant from the ferry terminal and the yacht club. Times of attendance are on display, and it is no use rapping on the window and grinning; the door only opens briefly at 8.00, 11.30 and so on. After due post-mortem, the papers that should have been issued at Ghyvelde will be filled in here, and promptly rescinded as the applicant declares his intention of leaving. Thereafter, feeling somewhat stateless and disenfranchised, there is little to do but wait for the weather.

Part of the outer harbour dries out, while the portion that does not is subject to a nasty swell. This can be crossed to visit a further non-tidal area, the Bassin Ouest. It contains a yacht club, but is usually crowded, so that the best course is to lurk surreptitiously in the Bassin Carnot. A visit to the Carnot lock house will elicit the times of opening, normally an hour-and-a-half before high water. *Donnez deux coups* (give two blasts) and a squad of blue-overalled operatives will open the gates. But do not overlook the traffic signals before dashing out, as there are often tugs bursting to come in. Thereafter, the way will be clear for the outer harbour and the English Channel.

Road and canalside frontier post at Ghyvelde.

A ROUTE THROUGH BELGIUM

Entering Dunkerque

Crossing the Channel

In *France – the Quiet Way* I described the traumas of bringing *Arthur* around from the Wash to the London River. That was a harder voyage than the one that followed, from the Thames across to Calais. In attempting the reverse, from Calais to the Thames, I was encouraged by *Secunda*'s performance on the IJsselmeer, and knew she could smash through seas that would stop *Arthur* dead. But I have also sailed in the English Channel enough to realize that weather conditions too uncomfortable for either vessel will often occur. We went through the same all-important stages of preparing the vessels, and listening to the Shipping Forecasts.

The most important matters to check on any motor boat putting to sea, are that she can withstand rolling and pounding without things breaking loose, and that the fuel filtration system is in good working order. The same waves that send pots and jam-jars all over the galley will stir up the sludge of generations in a fuel tank. It is vital to have good filters, to know where they are, and how their elements can be quickly cleaned or replaced. Fortunately *Secunda*, no doubt with the IJsselmeer in mind, was already so equipped, while *Arthur* still had the extra filters I had put in for the earlier crossings.

Secunda's cargo hatches had an ingenious locking mechanism, with a series of pins stuck downward through lugs on the steel coamings. Long steel rods could be passed through holes at the feet of these pins to secure them in place. We laid out a line as a handhold along the hatches and checked the anchor winch, a device of many brakes and handles, so that we would know how to lower the cable in a crisis. I had already made sure that the other end of the chain was secured with the traditional rope, which allows it to be released with a few hasty strokes of a breadknife, should this ever be necessary.

I wondered about the cabin windows, but decided, on balance, to leave them unshuttered. Timber blanks might have protected them, but these need to be accurately fitted. *Arthur*'s crew decided otherwise, lashing planks in place, one of which worked loose and cracked a pane. Many of the yachts I used to deliver had large windows every bit as exposed, but I never knew great seas to actually pound against them.

With our crockery all stowed, the table upturned and wedged, and an iron ration kit made ready in an old cardboard box, there remained the engine to check and the compass to think about.

The compass provides a particular problem on vessels made of iron or steel. For the previous *Arthur* epics we had used a hand-bearing instrument mounted at eye level on a timber upright. By taking various headings along a canal and comparing the readings against the course as shown on the map, I had effectively 'swung' this compass and plotted deviation curves. But the same method did not prove successful on *Secunda*. There was so much metal around that the only place an accurate reading could be obtained was out on the hatches forward of the wheelhouse, standing with a similar hand-bearing compass. This we would have to use.

Calms are difficult to predict. The Meteorological Office is reluctant to do so. Even when the sea is like glass all around the British Isles the broadcasts tend to speak of winds of 'Force three to four' which, if they materialize, are more than enough for craft like *Arthur*. The only thing to do is listen to all four BBC shipping broadcasts each day, write each one down, and compare the station reports with the forecasts issued previously. It then becomes possible to build up a picture and gauge the rate of change. I had started doing this as we entered the Canal de Furnes and, expecting to wait several weeks skulking around Calais docks, was startled to find an excellent forecast as soon as we arrived there. Lest anyone else should try a similar crossing, I would add, to all the customary cautions, the need for time to spare, weeks and weeks of it, for the weather is rarely so co-operative.

Up the beach at Holt's yard, Heybridge on the River Blackwater.

The number of voyages that have fallen foul because people were obliged to start through lack of time is beyond measure.

We left Calais at 4 a.m., with myself and Michael's son Philip aboard *Secunda*, towing *Arthur* on a very long line. The wind was light, raising a slight popple which was to die away as the trip progressed. Having crossed the tip of the Calais banks, which it is possible to do at high water in calm conditions, we laid a course for the South Goodwin light vessel. Looking back, I could see *Arthur* stubbing into the waves, with two tarpaulined figures at the helm. From time to time Rob shrewdly held his reading of the course aloft on the blackboard, for us to read through binoculars and check against our own.

There was one prolonged moment of doubt. The Channel is now divided into two main shipping lanes, south-going on the English side, northbound on the French. Craft like ourselves, crossing over, are asked to do so at right angles to these courses. Those crossing at an acute angle, or going against the flow, are increasingly being prosecuted; but there remain, lumbering about on this high-speed course, numerous vessels going the wrong way. We met one, a large tanker, which after sidling up the southbound track started homing in on the South Goodwin light.

One of the other rules of the sea is that vessels should not pass within a mile of a lightship. It agitates the occupants who, in this case, fired a rocket at the marauder. This set the tanker turning towards us, just as a ferry from Dunkirk came charging into the arena. Two little ships progressing at five knots with three hundred metres of line between them feel rather vulnerable in these conditions. Since it was by no means certain what the tanker would do next, and since one of the possible solutions was for the ferry to swerve, either through the lightship or through us, the only thing I could think of was to turn completely away. All this happened in very slow motion, as it often does at sea, but these situations build. As a result we turned in a complete circle, the ferry

went through where we might have been, and the tanker blundered off elsewhere. And once or twice in the action we had been across both swell and wash, causing *Secunda* to put in some heavy rolls, a reminder of what it might be like out there.

The rest was plain sailing. Deal Pier passed, then Ramsgate. By the time we had reached the North Foreland the sea was like glass. I had arranged a mooring near Maldon on the River Blackwater in Essex. *Arthur* was bound for Braunston, near Rugby and up the Grand Union Canal; and so, within striking distance of the Thames we cast off the tow and split. *Arthur* dwindled to a dot as we headed north across various flats and sands, picking our way between the shallowest patches, skirting an area of underwater concrete boulders, and passing close to the Shivering Sand Towers, relics of World War I.

With our forecast interpretation spot-on, it was an easy passage. The early afternoon broadcast confirmed that no hurricane was waiting to blast us; the forecast for Sea Area Thames was for 'winds light, variable', as favourable a prophecy as can ever be uttered. With the sea like a mirror, and visibility practically unlimited, the often hostile estuary became a navigator's paradise. It was possible to make every move on transits by keeping selected buoys in line, and we could see them all. By early morning we were off Brightlingsea, and since the mooring I had reserved involved drying out, quite literally up a beach, it seemed better to anchor for the night. There was a pleasant spot off the local yacht club, and for the first time ever under her new ownership, *Secunda*'s anchor was brought into play. Not having any marks on the chain at our disposal, Philip and I let out the lot.

We regretted this in the morning. Forty revolutions of the handle were as much as either of us could manage. We took it in turn; by the time the anchor was breaking out – the stage at which maximum energy and alertness are needed to handle the ship as she begins to drag on the tide – both of us

CROSSING THE CHANNEL

Stuck again, after returning from Holland, in a bridge modified with cement cladding, Number 79 south of Newport Pagnell.

were tottering. It was with stars before the eyes that I took the wheel and guided *Secunda* up to Arthur Holt's yard, just before the entrance to Heybridge Basin.

There were two other barges at Holt's, lying in what is popularly known as a 'mud berth'. I had arranged with James Macmillan, who looked after that side of things, to lie alongside them.

Very gallantly, James rowed out to greet us. Perhaps this was because *Secunda* had already penetrated the outer defences of moored yachts. As I realized later, I hadn't taken the best line of approach, but things always look different the first time. I threw a coil of rope into James' face, and soon we were alongside an old wooden Thames sailing barge, the *Ardwina*. Beyond that lay an attractive small motor barge, *Anny*, another refugee from the Netherlands.

Before we knew it, the tide had left us stranded, and a gangplank had to be arranged; also fenders to stop us demolishing a nearby shed, and many ropes, to every point of the compass. In the space of two hours the Blackwater Estuary had emptied of water, and muddy footprints appeared on the side-decks we had so lovingly washed each day. It was a place of different traditions.

Arthur Again

Her Majesty's Customs were kind, but formal, and to my relief confirmed that no importation payments were necessary. Our very first move after clearing was to set off for central England in search of *Arthur* and crew.

Philip and I found them chugging doggedly through a bridge on the Grand Union Canal, somewhere north of Leighton Buzzard. Robbie still puffed his pipe, Michael remained swathed against the elements. The awning had been dismantled because the bridges were too low and already a small boy had warned, as small boys are prone to do, that 'you'll never get through'.

During the period of my own ownership Bob, myself and several other friends had made an expedition up the Grand Union Canal, to see how far we could get. Although it was almost exclusively used by narrow boats, the Grand Union Canal is equipped with broad locks, capable of taking two narrow boats at a time, or single vessels with the beam of *Arthur*. In practice working with wider boats was never a success, because, it is said, the canal was too narrow for them to pass, and because one or two bridges were tight. In recent times the canal has been listed as 14 feet wide to Berkhamstead in the Chilterns and narrow thereafter.

In our first journey we had passed well beyond Berkhamstead and reached Northamptonshire. The two long tunnels, at Blisworth and Braunston, we had entered at dead of night, to avoid meeting other traffic, since we were scraping the walls on either side; but eventually we had stuck in a bridge farther towards Birmingham. I remember it

well, Bridge Number 103, connecting an empty field on one side with another on the other. We were an inch too large for it. A working party from the sundry other craft we had delayed eventually eased us through the bottleneck by hacking away a piece of towpath, and we had proceeded towards Warwick. Finally a bridge with a low arch prevented us going any further and we called it a day.

The Bridge 103 incident had been caused by a modern concrete edge sticking out into the channel, an unnecessary intrusion, in my view.

It was even more irritating now to find that several other bridges had become narrower during *Arthur*'s absence in France. We encountered several, with inches lost here and there by towpath rebuilding, realignment, or recent cladding of the arch in a skin of cement. By devious means, such as tilting the ship with planks or pumping the ballast tank, we were able to lever *Arthur* through; but I could not help recalling the new canal at Heerenveen, or the widening at Assen, to say nothing of the doublings on the Moselle.

It was a sobering, almost anticlimactic, experience to reach Braunston again. Michael had once run the boatyard there and the last fleet of narrow boats to ply on regular contract on the Grand Union Canal. We entered the old basin where they used to dock. From there, through a short cut, we entered the reservoir, now thronged with pleasure boats, and moored *Arthur* among them.

From Northwich, Cheshire where *Arthur* had been built, this 'ship' had travelled the Leeds & Liverpool Canal for thirty-eight years, before going around the coast to London. There had followed trips up the Grand Union and Thames, before the crossing to France; and after that the Moselle, the Rhine, Friesland, Belgium and now Braunston again. Mike subsequently handed the vessel on to Bill Fisher, another friend of mine, who in turn, after some further Grand Union trips, has sold *Arthur* too. I wish the new owners well: as the Bingley coal merchants James Glover & Company had once so kindly written to Michael, '. . . we wish you well with barge *Arthur*; she was always a good ship.'

Barges in England

The immediate and abiding impression on bringing a Continental barge to England is that the facilities are very poor. Whereas in Holland, Belgium, France or Germany mooring such a thing is a commonplace, often undertaken at no charge at all, keeping what are regarded in England as 'large' vessels is precarious and expensive. The English canal system is too small for them, the various docks bastions of unavailability and intrigue. A lot of money can be paid merely to enter the Thames above Teddington, where craft are now charged according to the surface area they occupy. There are few docks or tidal blocks, hardly any cranes, nobody with the facilities of the little yard at Staveren, which thought nothing of hauling a barge out sideways for a quick look, the odd repair, and putting her back in the water on the same day.

All in all, keeping a barge in England is a battle. For a lot of money the battle can be won. I would have dearly loved, for instance, to have kept *Secunda* in the old St Katharine's Dock, now a yacht haven, but it was too pricey for me. The most de-energizing feature of all is the amount of lobbying and enquiry needed to moor anywhere.

At Heybridge I became used to adjusting the moorings and washing off mud. These are disadvantages of being out in the tide. The good points are also numerous. The Blackwater and Maldon, a thoroughly ramshackle port, were the refuge of several surviving Thames sailing barges. None were any longer in trade, but a growing number had been rescued from dereliction and were sailing on charter.

Lying in an upper bunk in *Secunda*'s stern cabin, I had an unsurpassed view across the estuary. At low tide there were seabirds on the mud flats, at high water all manner of vessels jockeyed to enter Heybridge Basin, a freshwater haven too crowded to admit *Secunda* at that time. One morning at dawn I watched two barges under sail cross tacks, big bat-like shapes slipping by without a sound.

John Porter, a composer, who lived in *Ardwina* alongside, was an enthusiastic barge owner. Val, who was a teacher, and lived on *Anny*, had once worked as mate on the sailing barge *Kitty*. Both would ply me with estuarial lore. They had barge dogs and cats, who occupied a convoluted *demi-monde* of jealousies and intrigue. Stranded up the beach, I could watch Val beating past in her lug-sailed dinghy with Manx as crew, a great black booby of a retriever who might have won prizes had he not grown to an enormous size and been born without a tail. He was an obsessive bringer-back of lumps of wood, and could pester endlessly. The trick was to throw something so that it rolled under an upturned boat on the slipway. He would then cheerfully spend an hour or so waiting for it to come out.

Heybridge is a place of dogs and cats; occasionally there would be fights, usually between mongrels in the more crowded recesses of the nearby pub. More often Manx would run through the car park antagonizing Alsatians locked inside Jaguars.

One day a novel may be attempted about Heybridge; it has sufficient material for a rack of them. Likewise the story of raising the money to convert *Secunda*, of gathering together a group of partners, and of crossing to France yet again. *Secunda* was duly converted as a hotel boat, to a standard I had not dreamed of, and taken back to the Canal du Nivernais. Her new layout was based on drawings by my brother Peter, who with fastidious care had measured every detail of the new ship on that first-ever trip through the Friesland canals. Once, when we had to tow a sailing boat

clear of the mud in the polder channel, his drawings had blown away in the brouhaha. Undeterred, he had measured her all over again; and although *Secunda* changed her form considerably, and went back to ply in mountainous wooded country, I still find myself thinking wistfully of the Frisian meers, of cycling around to Hindeloopen on Sundays, and of the fields and watercourses on those wild windy days.

Cruising barge 'Secunda' — length 29.14m (95ft 7in); beam 5.00m (16ft 5in); engine, Gardner 6LW six-cylinder diesel.

a — passenger cabins; b — toilet and shower facilities; c — saloon; d — galley; e — crew's quarters.

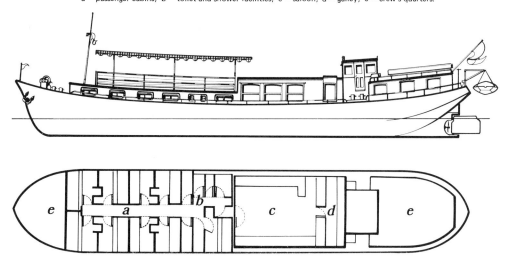

After conversion for the French canals

A klipper in France: repainting the name.

Appendix

Entry into Holland

Official requirements are few. Membership of a yacht club or kindred association will usually be accepted as evidence that a vessel is on a temporary visit only. The ship's Certificate of Registry should be carried on board at all times under the British regulations, but is rarely asked for in the Netherlands. Lest title to ownership should ever be doubted, it is prudent to carry some evidence, and if the vessel is unregistered application may be made to the Royal Yachting Association at Victoria Way, Woking, Surrey. The Association will issue for a modest fee an International Certificate for Pleasure Navigation.

If passing through France or Belgium, the registration papers or International Certificate will be called for. When travelling through Germany, some indication of competence may be required for those in charge of vessels over 15 tons displacement; but in at least one case registered tonnage has been accepted on the Rhine, on a converted barge deliberately measured to give her a low tonnage figure. As there is no mandatory Certificate of Competence for yachtsmen in Britain, and as other countries accept the certificates of their neighbours, an ambiguous situation can arise. A Yachtmaster's Certificate may be handy, if available; failing that, a formal looking letter from someone who can be represented as an expert, saying that the bearer is a good chap. In theory, the vessel must be certificated also in Germany, but a lenient view has once again been taken of those coming from abroad.

In the Netherlands the attitude is very lenient indeed, with no permits or passes, or driving licences, or indeed charges, save sometimes for mooring plus the odd token at a bridge or a random fee at one or two of the locks.

But at all times it is a wise precaution to carry evidence of cover for Third Party liability, and insurance documents issued in Britain should be amended to include the new cruising area.

Navigational Regulations

The only other official requirement in the Netherlands is that a copy of the basic navigation rules, the *Vaarreglement*, should be carried on board. Craft of more than 15 tons on the Rhine and its major branches should also carry the *Reglement van Politie voor de Rijnvaart*, which are very similar.

This requirement can be technically met by carrying on board the *Almanak voor Watertoerisme, Deel 1* (Volume 1), a softback book available from chandlers both in Britain and in Holland. For many this will be a gesture only, since it is printed in Dutch. An English translation of the *Vaarreglement* may be found in the *West European Pilot*, obtainable from N. V. Observator, Steenhouwerstraat 15, P.O. Box 7155, Rotterdam. Extracts are also published in Volume 1 of

Inland Waterways of the Netherlands by E. E. Benest. For those familiar with the International Regulations for Preventing Collisions at Sea much will be common sense, but the following is worth noting:

Pleasure craft must keep well clear of commercial traffic, and have no right of way.

On all save unpowered craft, the helmsman must be at least sixteen years of age, and capable.

Speed must be reduced near bridges and locks, or wherever the wash may cause damage.

Lock and bridge operation by boat crews is forbidden.

Engines should be shut off in locks.

When craft meet in narrow places in a current, the downcomer has precedence.

When craft meet in a current, the vessel going against the stream may hoist a blue flag or board on the starboard side of her wheelhouse to indicate that she wishes to pass starboard to starboard. Craft proceeding downstream hoist a similar signal to acknowledge. At night a white rapidly flashing light is substituted for the flag or board. (This is an exception to the basic rule that traffic keeps to the right.)

Books, Charts and General Literature

A good start may be made at the admirable Netherlands National Tourist Office; main address, 's-Gravenhage (the Hague) 2005, 17 Mauritskade, tel. 924551; London office, 2nd floor, 143 New Bond Street, London W1Y 0QS, tel. 499-9367. In addition to the usual maps and leaflets the office issues a brochure *Holland, Watersports Paradise*, containing much useful information.

North Sea Harbours, Calais to Den Helder by E. Delmar Morgan, published by Adlard Coles Ltd, is a useful pilotage guide to the approaches.

Frisian Pilot: Den Helder to Brunsbüttel and the Kiel Canal by Mark Brackenbury, published by Stanford Maritime, is a detailed pilot to the Dutch and German Frisian islands and mainland coast, and the approaches to the Kiel Canal, with harbour plans and photos.

Waterways in Europe by Roger Pilkington, published by John Murray, covers numerous European waterways entertainingly and in useful detail as to mooring places and facilities. Several Dutch routes are included, as is the German Rhine and Mosel.

Inland Waterways of the Netherlands by E. E. Benest, published by Imray, lists the salient dimensions of all Dutch waterways, with kilometerage tables and many valuable appendices and notes.

Holiday Cruising in the Netherlands by John Oliver, published by David & Charles, covers the Dutch system in a workmanlike style, with much useful detail on moorings, handling etc, written from the viewpoint of an experienced voyager in an auxiliary sailing cruiser.

Almanak voor Watertoerisme published by the ANWB, KNWV and NKB organizations in the Netherlands, includes in Volumes 1 and 2 respectively the regulations and details of harbours and locks, with opening times, addresses etc. Despite being written in Dutch, there is much that may be extracted from Volume 2, while Volume 1 should be on board all pleasure craft in order to comply with Dutch law.

The Netherlands by Max Schuchart, published by the New Nations and People's Library, is a most shrewdly written account of the history and contemporary affairs of the country.

Muirhead's Holland (and also *Muirhead's Belgium*) in the erstwhile Benn's Blue Guide series are well worth tracking down. Out of print but available second hand from time to time, they are packed with detail on every town, hamlet and corner house, and although last published in the 1960s, have dated little.

Michelin Guide to Germany is another excellent condensation.

All about the Rhine by Hans G. Prager, a Franckh's Pocket Guide Book, translated into English, covers the river from its source to Holland, with the emphasis on barge handling and the river life.

Many of these books may be obtained from specialist booksellers in Britain, such as Captain O. M. Watts of 45 Albemarle St, London W1; J. D. Potter Ltd, 145 The Minories, London EC3; Stanfords Ltd, 12–14 Long Acre, London WC2. Potters also maintain a large stock of British-published charts, and are agents for Dutch charts.

The following Continental maps and charts are important.

For the Rhine, the *Rheinkarte, Bodensee-Nordsee*, by Binnenschiffahrtsverlag GmbH of Duisburg-Ruhrort, a single sheet covering the entire river. This may be supplemented by the admirable Michelin maps of the country on the scale 1 cm:2 km, as sold in bookshops all over western Europe, and with such rudimentary equipment the prudent navigator will get by. Properly, however, a full *Rheinatlas* should be purchased at a local chandlery, but it costs in the region of £40 and the temptation to fall back on everyday road maps is very strong. The latter will suffice for the docile and well-controlled Moselle, together with one of the local strip-maps *cum* guides that are commonly available.

For the Southern Estuaries, four sets of coloured yacht charts (*Kaart voor Zeil en Motorjachten*) are published in Holland by the Hydrographic Service, with keys printed in both Dutch and English. Revised annually, they appear as four large-format books: 1803 – Westerschelde; 1805 – Oosterschelde and Veerse Meer; 1807 – Grevelingen, Krammer, Volkerak and Hollandsch Diep; 1809 – Hoek van Holland, Nieuwe and Oude Maas, Rotterdam etc.

For the IJsselmeer, yacht chart 1810; and for the Waddenzee, the area of the North Sea within the Frisian Islands off the northern coast, two yacht chart books, numbers 1811 and 1812, cover the western and eastern portions respectively.

For tidal flows, *Reed's Nautical Almanac*, the standard handbook for the British yachtsman, dispenses brief information on the River Schelde and Hook of Holland, and gives particulars of the outer entrances and flow in the North Sea, but inside the river mouths Dutch references are again necessary. These are *Stroomkarten*, tidal stream charts of the type where one card is moved behind another and arrows show up in little holes. Again published annually by the Dutch Hydrographic Service, these are also available in Britain. *Stroomkarten* numbers are: 1891 – Westerschelde; 1892 – Oosterschelde; 1893 – Volkerak and Grevelingen; 1894 – Haringvliet and Hollandsch Diep; 1895 – Hoek van Holland, Rotterdam, Dordrecht; 1896 – Waddenzee.

Both types of chart may be obtained from numerous chandleries and shops in the Netherlands, as well as the British sources listed.

Born's Schipperskaart, published by Born NV of Assen, is a good overall map of the country, showing locks and canals graded by size. It may be obtained from British chandlers or the shops listed above, and many Dutch shops.

ANWB *waterkaarten* are coded as follows:

A Groningen and North Friesland

B Frisian Lakes

C Northwest Overijssel

D Gelderse IJssel

E Randmeren

G Amsterdam – Alkmaar (with inset Alkmaar – Den Helder)

H Hollandse Plassen (Lakes)

I Vechtplassen (Lakes)

J Big Rivers, west sheet, Hook of Holland to Gouda, Goeree to Dordrecht

K Big Rivers, central sheet, IJsselmond to Wijk bij Duurstede, Moerdijk to St. Andries

L Big Rivers, east sheet, Wijk bij Duurstede to Lobith, St Andries
M Limburgse Maas
N Biesbosch
O Veerse Meer
P Vinkeveense Plassen
R Loosdrechtse Plassen
S Belgium and NW France

These may be ordered through a British shop or motoring organization, or from J. D. Potter. In Holland they can be obtained from ANWB offices, open from 8.45 to 16.45 on weekdays and 8.45 to 12.00 on Saturday. Addresses are:

Alkmaar Koelmalaan 16 *tel.* 02200-1 90 41
Amersfoort Arnhemseweg 16-18 *tel.* 03490-1 02 45
Amstelveen Kostverlorenhof 5 *tel.* 020-45 51 51
Amsterdam Museumplein 5 *tel.* 020-73 08 44
Amsterdam Surinameplein 33 *tel.* 020-17 31 35
Apeldoorn Loolaan 31 *tel.* 05760-1 37 10
Arnhem Bergstraat 2 *tel.* 085-45 45 41
Arnhem Het Dorp, Dorpsbrink 1 *tel.* 085-45 33 55
Assen Kloekhorststraat 44 *tel.* 05920-1 41 00
Breda Wilhelminapark 25 *tel.* 01600-4 24 50
Den Haag Wassenaarseweg 220 postbus 2200 *tel.* 070-26 44 26
Den Haag De Savornin Lohmanplein 10 *tel.* 070-68 56 50
Dordrecht Nicolaas Maessingel 200 *tel.* 078-4 07 66
Eindhoven Eizentlaan 139-141 *tel.* 040-11 81 55
Emmen De Weiert 84 *tel.* 05910-1 46 78
Enschede De Klanderij 130 *tel.* 05420-2 37 00
Groningen Ubbo Emmiussingel 27 *tel.* 050-12 50 45
Haarlem Schotersingel 117a *tel.* 023-26 02 50
Heerlen Apollolaan 146 *tel.* 045-71 78 33
's-Hertogenbosch Burgemeester Loeffplein 13 *tel.* 04100-4 53 54
Hilversum Noordse Bosje 1 *tel.* 02150-4 17 51
Hoogvliet Binnenban 6 *tel.* 010-16 41 00
Leeuwarden Lange Marktstraat 22 *tel.* 05100-3 39 55
Leiden Breestraat 142-144 *tel.* 01710-4 62 41
Maastricht Koningsplein 60 *tel.* 043-2 06 66
Middelburg Plein 1940, 6 *tel.* 01180-48.00

Nijmegen Berg en Dalseweg 22 *tel.* 080-22 23 78
Rotterdam West Blaak 210 *tel.* 010-14 00 00
Schiedam Parkweg 216 *tel.* 010-70 43 33
Terneuzen Kersstraat 3 *tel.* 01150-79 60
Tilburg Spoorlaan 396 *tel.* 013-43 40 45
Utrecht Van Vollenhovenlaan 277–279 *tel.* 030-91 03 33
IJmuiden Lange Nieuwstraat 422 *tel.* 02550-1 51 44
Zaandam Peperstraat 146 *tel.* 075-16 75 59
Zwolle Tesselschadestraat 155 *tel.* 05200-3 63 63

Suitable Craft

In *France – the Quiet Way*, I listed the basic attributes of vessels suited to Continental canals: a tough hull, preferably of steel to withstand the wear and tear of locks and walls; a single screw to avoid the damage that often ensues when craft with twin propellers pass close to a shallow bank when meeting a barge; a stern steering position for precise manoeuvring at lock entrances; and big, strong fittings for ropes, without any clutter to impede them.

A similar specification suits parts of Belgium, and to a lesser degree Germany and the Netherlands; but there conditions often correspond to those of a sheltered estuary (and in the IJsselmeer and at the mouth of the Scheldt, an unsheltered estuary). Seaworthiness is more of a requirement. Flared bows, a hindrance in the many locks of central France, become an asset in shedding waves; a powerful engine, something of a waste on a calm canal, is useful in beating through a chop; propeller and rudder gear need not be so well protected for locks are so rarely encountered, and are so large and well run, that almost any yacht will survive through careful fendering.

Thus craft that are not particularly suitable for France may prove a good proposition in the rough and tumble of these more varied waterways. Boating conditions of virtually every kind are to be found.

If a compromise vessel is to be sought, she is probably an iron or steel sailing craft of the traditional Dutch type, seaworthy enough to survive all manner of discomfort in the estuaries and meers, tough and shallow enough to explore the narrower remote canals, where the locks may be more frequent. She will have a mast that lowers easily, and leeboards rather than a deep fixed keel. She will also have a reliable inboard engine, not an outboard which is comparatively inefficient and harder to manage at locks and bridges.

In buying a second-hand barge, my own experiences, extensively covered in these pages, should give sufficient pointers. Reservations regarding hull and engine condition are obvious enough. The ship's papers, the *Meetbrief* and *Certificat van Onderzoek*, will give the vessel's history and indicate when she was last approved for trade; enquire also as to the terms of her last insurance, and whether hull inspections were a requirement. If they were, evidence of condition should be forthcoming from the last surveyor. If in any doubt, obtain an independent assessment, where necessary upon a slipway, after enquiry as to terms at the local barge yard. In particular check the beam of any commercial vessel approaching 5 metres. Any hull in excess of 5.05 metres beam will be in trouble if taken into central France.

If work is envisaged on a barge and she is to be taken away, it is worth considering having it done in Holland before departure. Dutch yards are held to be expensive, by virtue of the exchange rate, but they can be highly efficient and swift. Any specialized repair or conversion work is best undertaken there, or in Belgium where yards are also skilled. In France, alas, facilities are poorer, and many of the old barge yards have decayed.

Dimensions of craft are not so critical in Holland itself, where an alternative route may almost always be found if the *waterkaart* shows a particular one to be too narrow, shallow or having fixed bridges. In order to voyage elsewhere, and particularly into France, a draft of under 1.10 metres is really advisable. This is the practical limitation across the summit and at the southern end of the Canal du Nivernais. *Secunda*'s dimensions of 29 m length, 5 m beam and 1.10 m draft indicate the limits of the Nivernais. Her overhead clearance of 3.70 m with the wheelhouse up denotes the safe maximum on the majority of French and Belgian canals, although the facility to fold down the wheelhouse to a mere 3.00 m overhead clearance has been useful from time to time. The Canal de Bourgogne, for instance, has a tunnel with little greater clearance, the Nivernais a bridge at 2.97 m (give or take a few centimetres according to the adjustment of the water level in the canal). The Canal du Midi in the south of France, so long a bottleneck with its tight bridges and shorter locks, is being modernized as I write.

Hiring, and General Facilities

There are few better and more economical ways of exploring new water, or a different type of holiday, than by hiring a boat for a week or fortnight. Numerous hire craft are available in the Netherlands, few in Germany or Belgium. Because of the rigorous regulations in Germany, and the lack of them in the Netherlands, and because facilities are so good there, many German yachtsmen take their holidays on the Dutch waterways. In Friesland in particular, both motor cruisers and comfortable sailing cruisers are available. The lakes of Friesland, relatively sheltered and safe, provide an excellent sailing ground for those with modest experience, recalling the Norfolk Broads in the days before they became too densely crowded. Advertisements for boating holidays appear in such British magazines as *Motor Boat and Yachting*, while the Netherlands National Tourist Office will provide further pointers.

There are numerous yacht yards in Friesland and around

the shores of the IJsselmeer, and chandleries in most waterside towns. Launching sites for towed craft, fuel supplies and repair yards are usually located in or beside the many marinas. Similar facilities are to be found in the south, although on the Great Rivers the accent is more on barge supplies.

On the Rhine and Mosel facilities are fewer, symptomatic once again of the difficulty that German nationals experience in taking to the water. There are occasional barge chandlers on the Rhine, surprisingly few on the Mosel, and in both cases sheltered moorings can be hard to find.

In Belgium, the inland waterways are largely geared to the barge trade, with pleasure boating facilities confined to the Channel ports, and, on a small scale, to the Meuse.

Boat Handling and Equipment

In confined waters, 'holding back' can be all-important. It is almost always prudent to reduce the throttle setting at first sign of a hazard. With experience and practice one will know more precisely when to do this, but newcomers should seize an early opportunity to judge how a boat behaves at low speed. Most single engined craft turn in one direction when the engine is put astern. Such a turn can often be counteracted by applying full rudder and then giving a brief kick in forward gear. The same trick can be used to prevent a boat from drifting under wind or current – provided that sufficient space remains around and ahead to permit the stern to swing and provide water for the boat to move into.

It is also courteous and prudent to slow down when meeting another vessel in a narrow channel. The basic rule of the road is to 'keep to the right'. In passing barges, do not be too frightened and drive up the bank; if the other holds the centre channel in a narrow waterway, it is perfectly in order to pass within six feet, or less. If both craft do so slowly, there is little chance of their being sucked together as they pass, although it is usually safer to keep some power on. When overtaking it is customary to wait until beckoned forward from the wheelhouse; but this is a rare event in the Netherlands, where commercial craft move briskly.

On big rivers, and as a general rule, pleasure traffic keeps well clear. At locks barges are normally allowed to enter first. If there is a press of traffic at large locks yachts are generally invited in by loudspeaker last of all, to secure firmly astern of the barges.

If pleasure craft are waiting at a staging, they should moor reasonably close together to allow room for latecomers; but a crowd of vessels too near the lock gates is always dangerous. Apart from the danger of currents and eddies, there may be some behemoth waiting to emerge.

Dutch locks are usually gentle affairs within, competently and courteously managed. Yet another golden rule: take your time, whatever the psychological pressures. Lines should be 40 feet or more in length, even for the tiniest yachts, and each with a noose at one end. These can be placed over a bollard on shore and tended from on board, generally the safest method, although some yachtsmen prefer to double lines from boat to shore and back again, with slightly greater risk of a tangle.

Ropes should be made fast on board with figure-of-eight turns around cleats or bollards, but without any jamming hitches that may prove difficult to undo. In the case of larger heavy craft, such as barges and barge conversions, several turns (not overlapping) of a rope around one of the ship's bollards will produce more friction. With conventional rope, which is right-hand laid with the strands twisting in the same manner as a wood screw, it is the custom to wind it in a clockwise direction, both around bollards and when laid in coils on deck, where it should be put down to as large a circumference as space reasonably allows.

Ropework is the key to boat handling on inland

waterways. On small light yachts it has become a neglected art and such spectacles as winding a rope around arm and elbow, as for a clothesline, or tying the end of a coil around itself, are a commonplace. They make bargemasters wince. On commercial craft lines are always kept ready. If coiled in the hand, each coil is measured with a swing of the arms, working along the rope away from a fixed end. For throwing, a number of coils are held in the left hand, before carefully separating into two groups and transferring the outermost half to the throwing hand. In experienced hands, this ensures that the line pays out to the maximum. Knots are used as little as possible on barges, again for fear of jamming; round turns, figures-of-eight and the occasional hitch are all that are generally needed.

Ropes apart, standard yachting equipment will suffice in the Netherlands: a good weighty anchor with plenty of chain, a dinghy and possibly a light gangplank (although alongside moorings are common enough), fenders for locks, buckets, fire extinguishers and lifejackets as commonly prescribed, a good hooter (sounding as unlike a car as possible) for use at bridges, a spotlight perhaps, although night navigation is not to be encouraged, and a selection of flags, including a blue one about one metre square for 'wrong side' passing on the major rivers. The Red Ensign is the normal flag for British yachtsmen to display, unless authorized to fly a blue one, or for members of the Royal Yacht Squadron, the extremely rare but much-remarked-upon White Ensign. The national flag of the country visited is customarily flown at the starboard crosstrees, or some equivalent position if a boat has not got them; but the flag of Friesland is often flown instead in that part of the world, and is appreciated. In the Netherlands at least, there is little need for the mighty water hoses, Forth Bridge type planks and other specialized gear necessary on the waterways of France; but binoculars are useful for picking out marker buoys and bridge signals, plus perhaps a magnet to fish for these and other accessories should they tumble overboard.

Buoys and Beacons

Both the cardinal and lateral systems of buoyage have been employed on Continental waters, with the lateral system the more generally used on rivers and canals. However, in 1977 a new buoyage system, the IALA system, was introduced in European waters with basic changes, chiefly in the colour coding. Since both old and new systems may still be found, both are listed below, starting with the long-familiar types.

OLD SYSTEM

Port-hand markers (to be left to port of a vessel travelling inland from the sea):

Colour: RED

Starboard-hand markers (to be left to starboard of a vessel travelling inland from the sea):

Colour: BLACK

Middle Ground markers:
Main channel lies to right (for craft travelling inland from the sea):

Colours: RED + WHITE

Main channel lies to left (for craft travelling inland from the sea):

Colours: BLACK + WHITE

Channels of equal importance:

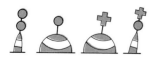

Colours: RED + WHITE

Other buoys:

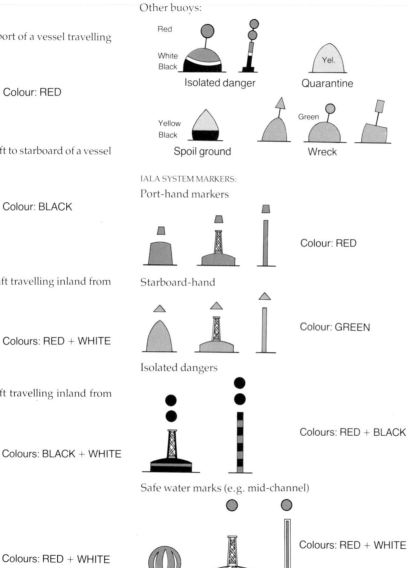

Isolated danger

Quarantine

Spoil ground

Wreck

IALA SYSTEM MARKERS:
Port-hand markers

Colour: RED

Starboard-hand

Colour: GREEN

Isolated dangers

Colours: RED + BLACK

Safe water marks (e.g. mid-channel)

Colours: RED + WHITE

Cardinal markers (topmarks indicate directional relationship to hazard):

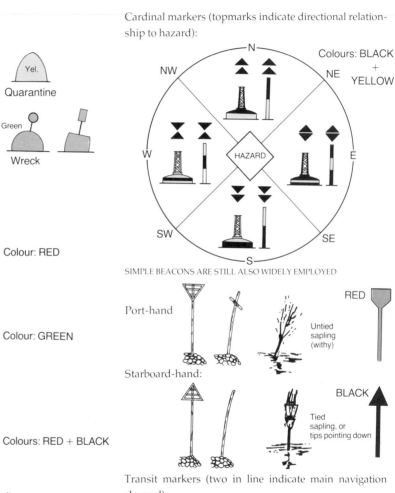

Colours: BLACK + YELLOW

SIMPLE BEACONS ARE STILL ALSO WIDELY EMPLOYED

Port-hand

Starboard-hand:

Untied sapling (withy)

RED

Tied sapling, or tips pointing down

BLACK

Transit markers (two in line indicate main navigation channel):

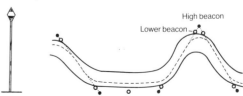

High beacon
Lower beacon

Sound Signals

One long blast

Attention, e.g. when calling for a bridge or lock, 4–6 seconds duration is customary.

One short blast

I am turning to starboard (to the helmsman's right), or **I aim to meet and pass you on the correct side** (i.e. to 'keep to the right').

Two short blasts

I am turning to port (to the helmsman's left); or **I aim to meet and pass you on the 'wrong' side** (i.e. to keep to the left).

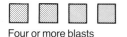

Three short blasts

My engines are going astern.

Four or more blasts

Danger/emergency: 'wake up.'

Two short, two long blasts

(between barges) **I wish to overtake on your port side.** Not acknowledged if in order; two short blasts in reply if overtaken vessel declines and wishes to be passed on her starboard side instead.

Two long, one short blast

(between barges) **I wish to overtake on your starboard side.** One short blast in reply if overtaken vessel wishes to be passed on her port side instead.

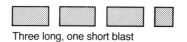

Three long, one short blast

(from barges in harbours or confined channels) **I am turning to starboard.**

Three long, two short blasts

(from barges in harbours or confined channels) **I am turning to port.**

In Fog

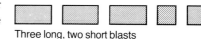

Three-tone ascending signal, repeated

(from commercial craft moving by radar) **Clear the channel/get to the side.**

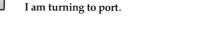

One long blast, repeated at 1 minute intervals

Vessel under way.

Two long blasts, repeated at 1-minute intervals

Push tug, or tug and barges under way.

Flag Signals

Blue flag on board, hoisted on starboard side by craft going upstream on major rivers that **wish to pass on 'wrong' side** (i.e. wish to keep to the left).
Craft going downstream fly a similar signal to acknowledge.

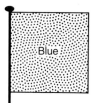

Blue flag at masthead (Rhine and subsidiaries): **Vessel overtaking.**

Red flag: **Vessel broken down or vulnerable please pass with care.** If shown on dredger, wait until withdrawn or pass on other side.

Red upper, white lower. Shown on the **safe side to pass** by dredgers *et al.*

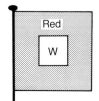

Red with white centre. **Compulsory** pennant to be flown at stem of **craft under way in Belgium.** Indicates craft wishing to progresss, e.g. at a lock, to distinguish from those waiting for a longer period.
Note: the same flag is flown at the masthead by **towed and towing vessels in the Netherlands.**

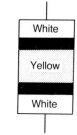

Yellow, black and white cylinder, hoisted on the mast. **Tug leading a train of barges.**

Yellow sphere hoisted on the mast. Last in a train of towed craft.

Notice Boards and Markers

NB: rectangular boards are for the waterways, circular notices for roads alongside.

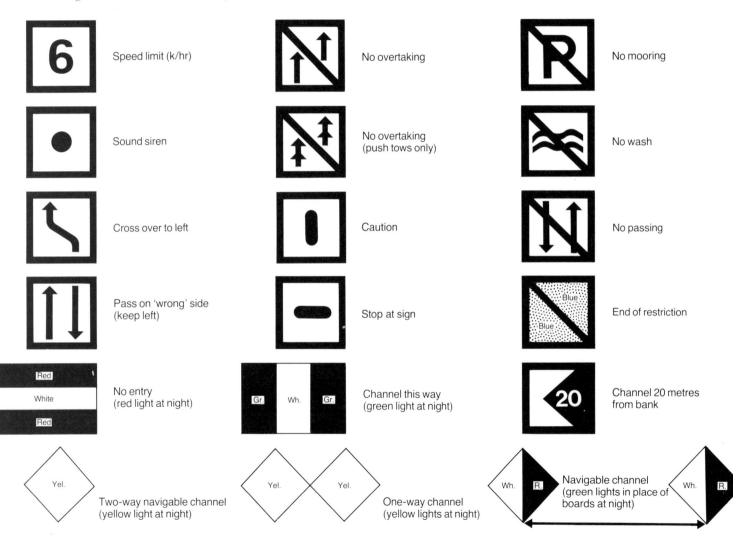

Speed limit (k/hr)

Sound siren

Cross over to left

Pass on 'wrong' side (keep left)

No entry (red light at night)

Two-way navigable channel (yellow light at night)

No overtaking

No overtaking (push tows only)

Caution

Stop at sign

Channel this way (green light at night)

One-way channel (yellow lights at night)

No mooring

No wash

No passing

End of restriction

Channel 20 metres from bank

Navigable channel (green lights in place of boards at night)

Index